Stage Voices

Stage Voices

*Interviews with 28
Theater Directors Worldwide*

STEVE CAPRA

McFarland & Company, Inc., Publishers
Jefferson, North Carolina

Library of Congress Cataloguing-in-Publication Data

Names: Capra, Steve, 1951– author.
Title: Stage voices : interviews with 28 theater directors worldwide / Steve Capra.
Description: Jefferson, North Carolina : McFarland & Company, Inc., Publishers, 2024. | Includes index.
Identifiers: LCCN 2023045523 | ISBN 9781476693248 (paperback : acid free paper) ♾
ISBN 9781476651187 (ebook)
Subjects: LCSH: Theatrical producers and directors—Interviews. | Theater—Production and direction—History—20th century. | Theater—Production and direction—History—21st century. | BISAC: PERFORMING ARTS / Theater / Direction & Production | LCGFT: Interviews.
Classification: LCC PN2053 .C316 2023 | DDC 792.02/320904—dc23/eng/20231006
LC record available at https://lccn.loc.gov/2023045523

British Library cataloguing data are available

ISBN (print) 978-1-4766-9324-8
ISBN (ebook) 978-1-4766-5118-7

© 2024 Steven Greechie. All rights reserved

No part of this book may be reproduced or transmitted in any form or by any means, electronic or mechanical, including photocopying or recording, or by any information storage and retrieval system, without permission in writing from the publisher.

Front cover image: © Mircea Moira/ Kozlik/ Shutterstock

Printed in the United States of America

McFarland & Company, Inc., Publishers
Box 611, Jefferson, North Carolina 28640
www.mcfarlandpub.com

With thanks to Ausra Simanaviciute, Alex Zixin Liu,
Rodolfo Obregón and Weronica Wozniak
for their interpreting services,
to Damon Emerson
for his translating services,
and to Ned Lynch, Grant Michaels and Diana Julian
for their support.

"We've not killed the theater yet
and I don't think we will."—John Doyle

Table of Contents

Preface 1

Oskaras Koršunovas	3	Li Ning	72
Nicholas Hytner	5	Gabino Rodríguez	76
Peter Schumann	12	Jorge Vargas	81
Malcolm Purkey	17	Marc Caellas	84
Judith Malina	21	Ivo van Hove	90
Robert Wilson	23	Krystian Lupa	95
Lee Breuer	26	Michael Blakemore	100
Richard Eyre	31	Robert Lepage	106
Anne Bogart	36	Kip Williams	112
Julie Taymor	42	Mauricio Kartun	118
John Doyle	48	Christiane Jatahy	124
Ping Chong	54	Stan Lai	129
André Bishop	60	Caitríona McLaughlin	135
Bartlett Sher	66	Robert Icke	142

Afterword 149
Index 151

Preface

I present interviews with 28 of the world's leading theater directors.

Theater is firstly a *live event*—everything else is up to the artist. It's enormously protean. It exhibits an enormous range of aesthetics, purpose and tone. The work of these directors exhibits this range—from the politics of Judith Malina and the puppetry of Julie Taymor to the expressionism of Robert Wilson and the high tech of Kip Williams.

It follows that the topics discussed are as varied as the theater—as varied as life. There are, of course, the obvious subject labels—rehearsal process, dramatic genres, politics. But we also discuss audiences, "bad productions" and as many other topics as there are avenues upon which to approach theater. And the ideas presented herein are, as well, as varied as thought itself—from Robert Icke's disappointment that we've been "bad guardians" of the theater, to André Bishop's celebratory words "We are living in a golden age of American theater." Still, there's a commonality. The 28 directors included in these pages are leaders in the theater, and they're all brilliant. Without exception, they're celebrated, honored, *fêted* internationally as the foremost directors in our theater world. That's a lot to have in common.

In editing the interviews, I've often retained the individual's characteristics of speech, including the redundancies, the digressions, and the idiomatic expressions (some of which translate better than others). It seemed important not to filter or screen the directors' words—to allow the reader access to the conversations as they unfolded.

This book is designed for education and entertainment. After all, when we're talking about theater, education is entertainment. Professionals and students will want to know what our leaders have to say, but the general audience is served here as well. Everyone who loves the theater will want to read what Caitríona McLaughlin has to say about female characters and what Lee Breuer has to say about Disney (or about Nietzsche, for that matter).

Preface

Not all these interviews are recent. Indeed, as of this writing we've lost two of our fellow travelers included here— Judith Malina and Lee Breuer. But an idea is not more valuable because it is more recent, and no interview is diminished by age.

I want to thank each director who took the time to talk with me. Their conversation, as the reader will see, was remarkable.

Oskaras Koršunovas (September 2007)

"Real theatre is produced
in the audience's imagination."

Oskaras Koršunovas founded the Oskaras Koršunovas Theatre, now also called the Vilnius City Theatre, in 1998. He's best known for productions such as A Midsummer Night's Dream *and* The Lower Depths. *His many awards include the Europe Theatre Prize for New Realities, the Vilnius St. Christopher Prize for Contribution to Culture and several Golden Stage Cross Awards. He's been honored with the Swedish Commander Grand Cross and the title Chevalier of the French Order of Literature and Arts.*

Steve Capra: *On your website, there's a quote: "No matter what the play is, every one of his productions has the same structure, peculiar to the dream and paradoxical thinking, which suggests a special combination of the abstract and verbal levels." Is the structure really the same for all your work, no matter what the script is?*

Oskaras Koršunovas: The structure and the performances are different, but of course, there are certain things that unify them. I was always interested in the kind of theater in which one is able to tell more than only words can tell. I'm talking about a certain inconstancy between what is said in words and what's going on, on stage—between the verbal text and the stage action. This paradoxical inconsistency produces a third dimension—and this third dimension is what theater really is.

SC: Your work is based visually. Do many audiences find it difficult?

OK: The visual itself is not really such a complicated thing for an audience. On the other hand, it depends on what kind of visual. I always try to avoid the kind of visual that only illustrates. If you use visual things only as an illustration of something, this kind of visuality means death to the theater. Real theater is not created in those ten or twenty square meters of stage, but real theater is produced in the audience's imagination. So you always must aim at the audience's

Oskaras Koršunovas (September 2007)

consciousness—and help it create images in their minds. If we try to achieve this very spectacular visual character on the stage, then we lose a very central part of what real theater is—instead of focusing on the audience's imagination. So you must leave on the stage only those things that might tickle the audience's—the spectator's—imagination.

SC: Doesn't the audience have to be very sophisticated for some productions?

OK: On the one hand, of course, the audience is quite sophisticated here. In Lithuania, we have a very strong tradition of director's theater, which is a kind of theater that philosophizes. In the Soviet period, theater in Lithuania was a kind of resistance, and it evaded censorship. The audience had to read in between the lines. In this way the tradition of this metaphorical theater was formed. On the other hand, the audience is always interested in what is a bit unusual or extraordinary. They are curious to find in the theater some experiences that might not always be so pleasant—but still they are quite curious. We've been touring a lot with our shows in many countries of the world, and we've discovered that the audience's response is more or less the same.

SC: You mentioned theater in the Soviet era. Since then, does theater address social issues more directly, more openly?

OK: Theater has to be metaphysically social. Theater always must be ahead of time and it must always address those issues that are not there yet, but are just germinating. If theater is only about the hot issues of the day—that you can read about in the press, or that people generally talk about—then it becomes boring, because it's not really what the real object is. Theater must address some hidden things, maybe things that are not named.

SC: Your website says you're interested in theater as confrontation. What response are you hoping for?

OK: In a certain sense, I try to provoke the audience. Real theater should provoke a certain conflict of the spectator, some kind of inner conflict. Particularly in this post–Soviet space. Theater for a long time replaced church—served as church. Maybe the audience now expects from theater that it will continue to confirm its beliefs. But real theater shouldn't be like this. It should like ripple the water and put all those long-established dogmas and values under doubt, and in this way create this inner conflict.

The theater is a kind of public space, and in this public space there are two groups of people—the audience, and the actors on the stage. Those actors should speak about things that are not officially sanctioned or officially established. Because only in this way can they be interesting or produce this conflict. If they talk about things that are already established or sanctioned then this theater is not really interesting. The essential thing is that some kind of conspiracy takes place between the actors and audience, because the audience must also understand what this whole thing is about. A lot depends on their response. If this conspiracy really takes place, then theater happens.

Nicholas Hytner (July 2008)

"I think it's necessary to be politically involved. I don't think it's necessary to have any explicitly stated political program. I think it's necessary to be politically skeptical."

Sir Nicholas Hytner was the director of the National Theatre, London, between 2003 and 2015. He was previously the associate director of the Royal Exchange Theatre, Manchester. He has directed productions in every genre, from opera and musicals to straight modern drama and Shakespeare. Some of his most important successes have been productions of Miss Saigon, The History Boys *and* The Magic Flute. *His many honors include two Tony Awards, two Drama Desk Awards and three Olivier Awards including the Society of London Theatre Special Award.*

Steve Capra: *There used to be a lot of talk in the States about how you had a national theater here in the UK and we didn't in the US. What does it mean to be a "national theater"? Is it more than a name?*

Nicholas Hytner: I think it means something different in every country that has one. We are the *johnny-come-lately* of national theaters. It was long in coming, and I think that's largely to our advantage.

We were certainly conceived on the model of a Continental national theater, but right from the beginning, when the idea was first mooted by the playwright Harley Granville Barker and the critic William Archer at the end of the 19th century, the notion was that it would *not* be a theater for the cultural elite but a genuine part of the social and

Nicholas Hytner (July 2008)

intellectual life of London, and genuinely popular. And in that respect, it is specifically in the English tradition.

The English theater has never been a court theater—it was conceived as a popular theater. The German and French theaters, by contrast, were court theaters at their inception. We look to the French and German theaters for a kind of institutional model, but we bring to them a determination to be public and to reflect here, on the South Bank, what the theater did on the South Bank at the end of the 16th, beginning of the 17th century—they aimed to have widespread appeal, to play for everybody, to challenge as well as reflect, to be vaguely disreputable. It's very important that the theater is on the South Bank. The Elizabethan theaters were on the South Bank because the city fathers wouldn't have them in the city. You'll notice I use "English" and "British" interchangeably. That is one of the most fluid and least defined aspects of our national theater. Are we the British National Theatre? Are we the English National Theatre? There is now a Scottish National Theatre, which nevertheless doesn't seem to me to suggest that we have no responsibility north of the border.

SC: Then you see English culture as one culture and you have no concern—or fear—of being local. After all, most people in the UK can't get here easily.

NH: Well, geographical ubiquity is impossible anyway. It's what gets on the stages that makes it national—not how widely we travel geographically. Much more interesting than how far we travel is what we think *national* means, generation to generation. It means something completely different now than what it did in 1963, when the National Theatre became a reality. Both what *national* meant and what *theater* meant would have gone more or less unchallenged in '63. There are much more contentious—creatively contentious—ideas now. The country has changed completely. London, as a crucible for the rest of the country, has changed completely. In 1963, you might have been able to reflect back a nation that was much more homogenous, and a theater that was much more agreed on being part of a grand, literary tradition. You can do neither now—and that's greatly to our advantage.

SC: Is it necessary then to take a political position?

NH: I think it's necessary to be politically involved. I don't think it's necessary to have any explicitly stated political program. I think it's necessary to be politically skeptical.

Nicholas Hytner (July 2008)

SC: Well, if you're a popular theater, doesn't that imply a political position?

NH: There are things that theater can do in the political realm that are specific to the theater. That's what we need to do. Anybody can take a political position—that seems to me to be a fairly narrow furrow for a theater to plow. We want to engage an audience in a fully humanized, fully ambiguous, fully imagined examination of a political situation in its widest sense. It's not our job to look at what's exercising Parliament and perform plays on those issues. It's not an *issue* theater. But if there is something of burning public interest that feels like it might be illuminated by what the theater can do, then it's necessary for us to get involved. That can take many, many forms. Most obviously in recent years, when this country and yours were involved in fighting a war in Iraq which was extremely contentious, we were able, by producing *Henry V,* to use a play to reflect light on a current situation in way that was not obvious and in no way unambiguous. By taking a play written in 1599 about a war of dubious legitimacy, we were able to create a dialogue with a war that was happening 400 years later. That's interesting! That's theatrical!

At the same time, we commissioned from David Hare a play [*Stuff Happens*] that was specifically about the build-up to the Iraq war. He made no effort to conceal that he thought the war was a terrible mistake. But the play itself was much less concerned with arguing a political position than it was in examining, in all its human ambiguity, the situation and the people who found themselves maneuvered into—and maneuvering each other into—a series of events that had terrible human consequences. It's the unpredictable, unanalyzable emotional undertow of great social issues that comes alive on the stage. It's an establishment cliché that audiences come together to be told what they think already. I'm not sure audiences come together to be told what to think, or even to worry about what to think. I think audiences come together to explore emotionally, at a level beyond rational political analysis, what it feels like to be collectively human and caught up in events which appear to be beyond individual control. That's what the theater does. That's what makes it *public.*

SC: Not to be skeptical, but does it have an effect, in terms of votes?

NH: I don't think it's *remotely* part of our business to be telling people how to vote! We're not politicians! I don't think that is the way in which art gets politically involved. I don't think anyone writes a novel to

Nicholas Hytner (July 2008)

tell people how to vote. A presidential candidate might write an autobiography hoping that he might solicit people's votes, but nobody's writing a *play* in order to solicit a vote. That's not what art does.

SC: In light of the fact that there are film and television, can theater have the influence—whether political or personal—that it had for Ibsen's audience?

NH: Well, I think it can. It is precisely because theater is live and real, and because it involves real human interaction that it can continue to have what you call *influence*—what I might call a profound effect. There's something irreplaceable about the genuine interaction in real space and real time between a person on a stage and people in an audience. In Norway, in the 19th century, there was little else available in the way of mass entertainment, so those who went to the theater must have received it in a context different from those who go now. But I can't imagine that any more people went then than go now. Still, people go—still, people see the plays of Ibsen.

SC: I'm interested in the way theater reflects its own nation, while on the other hand Miss Saigon *and* History Boys, *for example, have been so successful outside of the country. What am I to make of that—that the great musical hits of the past twenty years have been international? It concerns me that it's theater that's no longer reflecting a specific culture.*

NH: Well, we couldn't have this conversation in France. They wouldn't know what you were talking about, because a French playwright, a French theater director, would assume—I'm going to generalize but there's more than a grain of truth in this generalization—would assume that the stage is an arena for reflecting the interior world of the playwright, the essentially literary imagination of the playwright. There *isn't* really a public theater in France. You speak to French theater people, and they're either envious or, occasionally, contemptuous of a theater that is as socially engaged as the British theater effortlessly is.

You bring up *History Boys*, which turned out to been enormously popular play because it struck chords elsewhere in the English-speaking world. But was it socially engaged? Yes, it was fantastically socially engaged! Why was it successful? Because it was the product of a humane literary and theatrical imagination. It was popular because it put on stage a group of people with whom an audience were very, very happy to spend two-and-half hours. But it was a terrific play not just for those reasons, but because it was urgently concerned with our relationship to our past, with the meaning and uses of literature, and with the purpose of education. It was written by an English playwright who is never particularly concerned with whom he's addressing—who always assumed there are people who want to listen, but who had no idea that what he was writing would be vibrant for audiences outside of this country. It was a quintessentially National Theatre play in that it was popular and entertaining, and its concerns were, in a very broad and profound sense, deeply political.

SC: *That's encouraging, because I worry about theater losing its definition specific to a country. You've said for example—I think it was in a BBC special—that Brecht and Beckett influenced world theater.*

NH: One conversation that we hold less successfully than Olivier did is a conversation with the contemporary theaters of our continental neighbors. *That* is a *very* interesting conundrum! It's because our theaters have travelled off in such different directions. The plays that come out of the contemporary German, French, Italian, Spanish theater travel much less successfully than they used to. It might encourage you that despite of, or maybe *because of* globalization and the European Community, there is no pan–European theater culture. Or if there is, we are really on the outside of it.

We have much better dialogue between our theater and other English-speaking theaters. Our dialogue with the Irish theater and the American theater has always been extremely fruitful and extremely interesting. It would be fair to say the American theater and the Irish theater keep in touch with us and each other and the same way that we do—always have! *Always* have!

SC: *Without losing their sense of identity.*

NH: We're gonna take the Steppenwolf production of *August: Osage County.* That's an essential part of a continuing theater exploration. We can't put up walls and say, "We're only going to show you English theatre!" We'd stop knowing what it was to be English! What you look for is what's the same and what's different. That's why you go to the past—what's changed, what hasn't changed. You put on *Henry V,* and you find out that there are some aspects of Tudor and medieval warfare and diplomacy that are entirely remote, and some which are completely unchanged. The way men and woman fought for each other was the same twenty-five hundred years ago—the gods they believed in, completely different—the food they ate, completely different—the fact that they got hungry, the same.

You mustn't confuse a genuine dialogue between individual

Nicholas Hytner (July 2008)

national cultures with specifically-created global product—which I'm not gonna knock! I'm not gonna knock the Pixar animated films! I watched that last Pixar film, *Ratatouille*, and I think that is as good as movie gets. It's a brilliantly confected piece of global entertainment! But does it have more or less value than something from Spike Lee? No. It's just that they're looking for something different.

SC: Can we talk about the specifics of directing for a minute? How do you manage to approach Twelfth Night *and* Miss Saigon *and* History Boys *and be so successful in all of them? It would seem that the whole premise of something technical, like blocking, would have to be different.*

NH: Well, no, I think that the basics are the same. Truthful acting is truthful acting—a story's a story. How you stage a show, how you block a show, how you create a world... How you make sure that things ebb and flow, that you provide an audience what it needs in order to make up its mind how it's gonna get involved. Those actually are the same.

SC: But when you block to reveal the psychology of the characters in History Boys, *certainly that's not the same as blocking, creating a stage picture, in* Miss Saigon *to make us enjoy spectacle.*

NH: No, but there's an element of spectacle in *History Boys* as well. I'm not going to say *History Boys* is the best play I've ever directed, but it's my favorite of recent years. It involved, as directing always does, an element of teaching, because I was working with a lot of quite young actors. It involved the processes that *all* directors go through, which attempts to unlock a text and to find a way of making it, on the one hand, spontaneous, and, on the other hand, delivered in such a way as to include an audience in its literary richness. That process is not dissimilar from the kind of process you would go through if you were directing *The Importance of Being Ernest* or *The Man of Mode* [George Etherege, 1676], or indeed, *Twelfth Night*. It's something which those who work firmly in the English literary tradition—or the Irish literary tradition, or the American literary tradition—are no stranger to.

But *The History Boys* also involved some very specific technical challenges. The very first thing I thought when I read that play was "Hang on a minute! This is a series of seminars! This is a series of lessons! How am I gonna keep that theatrically alive?" The next technical challenge was that it's *not* a series of classroom scenes—there are other scenes too. There was the purely scenic challenge of seamlessly getting from one place to the next. The answer to that was those video scene

Nicholas Hytner (July 2008)

changes. They gave to the play an impression of much greater movement than it would otherwise have had, and they covered scene changes which would otherwise have been very boring. And, more important, they expanded and defined the world of the play. Those totally nuts-and-bolts technical things are the same whatever you're doing.

I am very conscious—I think you are *inevitably* conscious—of where any play fits within a theatrical tradition. I find myself most useful, honestly, with plays that require both a certain degree of spatial expansiveness and a degree of literary extravagance.

SC: *Those of us who work Off Off Broadway in New York, doing bold theater, progressive theater, political theater—we have no connection with Broadway or the West End, or even regional theater. How can we hope to fit into that? Is there any hope of assimilating our work into the larger theatrical consciousness?*

NH: From my observation, it's hard to be part of a serious American theater. There are plenty of British groups like yours out in our streets at the moment thinking "How the fuck do we get ourselves noticed by the National Theatre?" There is no institutional reason why not. There is no endemic reason why not. Over the last five years, the number of artists that we've engaged with—who, because of the taste of my predecessors, would not necessarily have found themselves in the National Theatre before—is high. Some of them have been theatrically out of the mainstream, some of it has been politically out of the mainstream, but there is no institutional reason, no economic reason, why you can't come and play the National Theatre.

You'll never play Broadway because all those people who come, spend two nights at the Marriott and eat in the restaurants, are not gonna come see your show. Does that say anything about your show? No—all it says it that you can't get 250,000 people to pay a hundred and twenty dollars to come see it. Why do you care?

SC: *Well, I'd like Broadway to be more challenging. I'd like Broadway to affect society.*

NH: You're wanting the wrong thing. What you're gonna want is some shift of perspective in the American theater that puts Broadway where it should be. Those who produce in the West End have a harder job than I do, but West End is neither the seal of quality nor a mark of influence or importance. Not at all! It's just there, as part of the wider ecology.

I fear that those whose business is Broadway have a vested interest not only in being economically productive, not only in being a branch of the P.T. Barnum entertainment industry, but also in proclaiming their own creative and theatrical importance, It is so interesting to talk to our Chicago colleagues for whom that doesn't register. If you're making theater in Chicago, what happens to be making money on Broadway is of much less interest than it is to someone who's making theater in New York.

It's not so much what Broadway *is* but what Broadway *stands for*. Broadway's terrific! It's glitzy! It's exciting! We love it when our shows go to Broadway. But for us, it's.... What did it say about *The History Boys* that it played Broadway and made a profit? Just that it was very surprising that that play which seemed so parochially English turned out to have wide international appeal. It was great that the National Theatre made a bit of money out of it, but did it make it *important* to us? No. No, what made it important was that we thought it was a good play.

Maybe it's just that we're terrible *snobs* here. Far more people go see *Dirty Dancing* at the Aldwych than will see the show that Katie Mitchell's just about to bring into the Cottesloe—*some trace of her*—which is right out on a theatrical limb, a weird meditation on Dostoyevsky's *Idiot*. Far, far more people will see *Dirty Dancing*. Does anybody here worry about that? Not for a second! Are we being snobbish about the coachloads who go see *Dirty Dancing*? Have I any objection to the fact that the coachloads prefer to see *Dirty Dancing*? No! Would I even *suggest* to those people that they might be better off seeing Katie Mitchell's meditation on Dostoyevsky's *Idiot*? No! They're probably having a better time at *Dirty Dancing*! Good for them!

Peter Schumann (May 2009)

"Preaching to our own community, if you want to call it that, is actually very valid. It shouldn't be looked down on, because they need us."

Peter Schumann founded Bread and Puppet Theater in 1963 after working as a dancer and sculptor in Germany. His Cheap Art and Political Theater *combines politics with vaudeville. The company is known for its use of large puppets and masks; its residence is in rural Vermont and it tours extensively. Among other honors, he's been awarded a*

Peter Schumann (May 2009)

Guggenheim Fellowship, the Herb Lockwood Prize in the Arts, the Erasmus Award (Netherlands), the President's Award from Puppeteers of America and an Obie Award for Lifetime Achievement.

Steve Capra: *How has your worked changed since you started?*

Peter Schumann: Well, I started on the fifties in Germany and then I came to the states in '61. The first thing I did in the states was in that first winter—I participated in the Living Theatre's and the War Resistance League's *General Strike for Peace* with a piece I had done in Germany. I see what happened as coming out of what I did in Germany, being a war child and living like a refugee for two or three years in my childhood, and then making an art that started with sculpture and music. That became dance and then, logically, became puppetry. I was very politicized by living on the Lower East Side in New York City My sense that art needs to be available, needs to be cheap—or *dirt cheap* as we say—to be out in the street and not to be elitist—that comes from living in that slum. Seeing that what the fine arts were doing was so disconnected from people's lives… I didn't want to go that way.

So the changes that happened to us were in the politics of the country. First we became aware in the early 60s about this horrible war in Southeast Asia—then later on what happened in South America, supporting dictators. The whole school book history version of this grandiose democracy collapsed pretty totally. Instead, one slowly accumulated enough of what America really is in the world that … [*laughing*] I wish I could convey these things to Obama, but I guess I can't! I won't have a chance!

That then was confronted in the 70s with some entirely different experience—moving to the countryside and living among country people. Learning how to live cheaply in the countryside means all sorts of things—gardening, chickens, and the rest of it…. That overwhelmed us for a few years. Then we became a part of the countryside. Now we look like part of the jungle of Vermont! The politics are dictated to us by circumstance and by current events. That's a long answer for a short question.

SC: That's an interesting answer! Do you have a political position? Are you a dissident…

PS: The only way I could define that would be to say that I'm an anarchist if I take a look at the existing politics.

SC: In an interview on your website you said that the camp at the Circus in Vermont became a hangout certain types of kids who collected there and get drunk. How do we avoid that when we're in the counter-culture?

Peter Schumann (May 2009)

How do we pacifist anarchists avoid the violent anarchists—the irresponsible people?

PS: We tackled that for quite a while because we had massive spectacles here that were attended by tens of thousands of people. We just couldn't handle it anymore. As soon as we became big we became automatically part of an American style of mass culture that we had no control over.

Our plays, even for a very large audiences, were always *unelectrical*—unamplified. We tried to make use of the existing circumstances, the weather, the acoustics, as they were—in the gravel pit or in the forest. We didn't want to amplify ... the whole idea of a big electrical unit moving into a tent ground right next to us, making it loud and driving the kids crazy... The secondary part of our political performances was the normal washed-out American mass culture phenomena which we had no way of penetrating. I mean, we moralized with them; we talked with them; we walked around.... We liked the kids; we were friends with them.... But their manners were educated by something very stronger than us—the mass culture, which is a money culture and which has a grip on the kids that's pretty terrific.

SC: So you're avoiding that by holding smaller performances?

PS: Yeah, we decided to simply stop the big spectacle—it happened only on two days here—and to spread the two days over a whole summer. That seemed to work, because now our audiences are of a size that we can manage.

SC: Peter, does your theater have a political effect? Or are we preaching to our own community?

PS: Well, the preaching to our own community, if you want to call it that, is actually very valid. It shouldn't be looked down on, because they need us. They don't have much in the mass culture that they can go by or enjoy. So just the gathering of people coming here, attending performances, even partaking in them—that is a service to the community, here in Vermont. In the city, it's a little different.

On the other hand, I do think there are unmeasurable effects in—in—in what?—in the brains of the beholders, that can't be made into statistics.

SC: Your work has certainly had a lot of influence around the country. But, at the same time, I don't see political street theater in every city—and I'd like to. Why is that? I would think that the community would need street theater and would need a political discussion of—

Peter Schumann (May 2009)

PS: It does, yeah. There was an upsurge of political street theater at the start of the Iraq War. A lot of those were people who had worked here and then gone home to Midwest or far West or down South—wherever they came from—they started their own groups. There was a lot of strong and interesting political theater all of a sudden. But the cops immediately reacted quite fiercely to all of this. In Philadelphia, they pre-emptively arrested our friends in their studio, destroyed all their puppets, took their tools away, before they could even go into the street with them. Similar things happened on the West Coast and in Chicago. There are many examples of extraordinary actions by police. As you know, in New York any cop can stop you if you wear a mask for disguising your face. Any cop can stop a parade that has a pole in it that might be used as a weapon. If you have a metal pole ten feet long with an American flag on it, you can carry that. *That* is not dangerous to anybody.

SC: Are you still running across police harassment as you tour?

PS: Oh we do... We sure do ... the normal police harassment... They're forbidding us things and ... totally illogical.... That happens all the time.

SC: Are you received the same way if you're in Asheville, or Atlanta, or New York?

PS: No, it is different from one community to another. The company just came back. They had very good experiences down there in North Carolina, South Carolina, Virginia, and in the coal-mining districts, Kentucky and so on. It's always hard to gauge. The host is always very important, what connection you have ... whether you are in a unionized area for people who are in the mines, or whether you are just working for hippie groups, or university campuses... All of this is quite different, one from another, so it's hard to generalize.

SC: Do you tour outside the country?

PS: We do, yeah.

SC: How are you received?

PS: Again I couldn't generalize. We have had a great reception in Italy. In Russia, not so great. Now we are going to Taiwan and China—that seems to be going pretty well.

SC: I saw your performance outdoors at Lincoln Center, The Divine Reality Circus Comedy, *which absolutely terrific. There were storks with bombs in their mouths and there were blackbirds with staffs... I could*

Peter Schumann (May 2009)

relate a lot of that to society and to politics, but there was some of it that I didn't understand. Am I supposed to understand everything and be able … be able to refer it—

PS: [*laughing*] No, because visual things have their own power and are not necessarily translatable into what we call *understanding*. By *understanding* we usually mean something *verbal*, something we *verbally* understand, but often our brain—or our eyes or our ears—can perceive things and understand them quite well, but wouldn't be able to put that into words. It's like music. And the same thing is true of sculpture or painting, or of any visual effect.

SC: I'm interested in how theaters like yours manage. I know that you've received money from the National Endowment for the Arts, but you've said that you don't like to write grants. How do you keep it together? How do you keep the theater going?

PS: Well, we actually have accepted Council for the Arts money only very few times, for special occasions—usually not even projects that the theater did, but that some offspring, some student of the theater did on his own and needed us as an umbrella. We decided in the beginning, when we started the theater, that we would not make our living either out of Council money or governmental money or grant money. We wanted to make a cheap form of theater that wouldn't be built from a budget, but just from scraps and garbage. And we have pretty much stuck to that.

SC: That's an extraordinary accomplishment—that you manage to do that.

PS: It's hard. It means that we have very fast turnover. People live under not-so-easy circumstances for a short while and then they get burned out. And then you end up doing everything over with the next people.

SC: So your income is fees from your touring performances.

PS: Yes… it's what people put in the hat. We don't charge, but we have a hat out for collection. It's only possible when you don't have a big overhead for administration and all those things.

SC: What do you see in the future for Bread and Puppet?

PS: A summing up of many shows. We do so many different shows every year. When I ask people what they remember of these shows, it's so confused. People get these shows truly confused one with the other.

So what we're really working on is an underlying show. Instead of working on these separate theme shows, we might as well make *a whole world show*. Everything else becomes a little excerpt of that.

Malcolm Purkey (April 2011)

"There's a political theatre that's political in its refusal to be political."

Malcolm Purkey was the director of the Market Theatre (now called the John Kani Theatre) in Johannesburg, South Africa, between 2005 and 2013. He's most noted for workshop-based theater, and for popular productions of The Threepenny Opera. *Other noted productions include* Ain't Misbehaving *and* The Girl in the Yellow Dress *(2011). He's been honored with the Breytenbach Epathlon for Best Director and the Olive Schreiner Award for Dramatic Literature, among other awards. In 2014 he became dean on the South African School of Motion Picture Medium and Live Performance, Johannesburg.*

Steve Capra: *Can we begin with Marianne Oldham's comments on* The Girl in the Yellow Dress? *[Miss Oldham was cast in the Market Theatre Production]. She said there were different reactions in different places in South Africa.*

Malcolm Purkey: We started at The National Festival of the Arts in a small town called Grahamstown. The audience that comes are very much festival-goers and have a particular quality as a festival-goers, so they were probably very direct, very willing to give standing ovations. We then went to Capetown which is very different. The white South Africans living in Capetown are the kind of audience you might expect in a British theater. There's still quite a strong British tradition, a certain attitude to language, a certain attitude to performance and a certain attitude to plays. And *The Girl in the Yellow Dress* actually fed into some of that attitude. It's about the relationship between an English teacher in Paris who encounters a black seeming Congolese man as a student. The real content of the play is the relationship between Europe and African as seen through a South African writer's eye. So that's Capetown.

Johannesburg—where we played two very long seasons, very successfully—is really a significant African city. There's a new generation, post-apartheid generation, newly educated, who are young and black

Malcolm Purkey (April 2011)

and open—and that generation has become very important to the Market Theatre. So we get at the Market Theatre a much more mixed audience, a much more dynamic, urban audience with strong dynamics between black and white.

SC: Were any audiences uncomfortable?

MP: The Market Theatre was founded as an open theater, meaning it bucked the laws of apartheid. It was open from the beginning in terms of audience and performance—within beats of its founding, it had black and white on the stage, black and white in the audience. On the one hand we have this very mean, ugly apartheid keeping power and control by the most brutal means. On the other hand we have these pockets of openness. Our audiences at the Market have been comfortable with one another for thirty-something years.

SC: And with the play?

MP: They've clearly liked it a lot, in the sense that they were on their feet almost every night.

SC: Were any of the audiences at all uncomfortable with the material?

MP: Some of this material is always designed to cause discomfort. The Market Theatre's mission from the beginning was not so much to be a political theater but to—in the words of Athol Fugard—bear witness. Our audiences at The Market Theatre expect to be challenged whether you're white or black—*according* to whether you're white or black—and, in a sense, to enjoy each other's discomfort in a very complex way.

SC: Could we speak about political theater? Do you think that all of the theater that you produce—or all theater—is political or overtly political?

MP: There are many different kinds of political theater. There's a political theater that bears witness but that avoids the descent into solemnity. To quote Brecht, theater that you can't laugh *in* is a theater to be laughed *at*.

There's a political theater that we in my own company were engaged with in the '70s and '80s. Aspects of the company were engaged with union theater. The task there was to use the theater on the shop floor, or in the rallies, or in the churches and union halls, in order to politicize and confront a generation of working class people, to engage in the revolution. Then there's a political theater that's political in its refusal to be political, if you like. A lot of theater in South Africa was paying homage to Britain, in some act of complicated colonial subservience. That theater would denigrate the more overt political theater.

My view is that the task of theater is to bear witness, to reflect our lives back to ourselves. The theater has to compelling, it has to be entertaining, it has to be funny... In the words of Peter Brook, it has to tumble towards us with all its images competing—its images, its feelings, its thoughts, its language, its dynamic—all competing to reach us first.

SC: Is it expected to have a political effect?

MP: You mean is meant to cause the revolution?

SC: Yes.

MP: When a hundred thousand people sing revolutionary songs and dance the *Toyi-Toyi*, which is kind of a war dance—that's art and culture directly involved with making the country ungovernable, which was one of the principles of the revolution. In that sense art and culture can bring down the state. Whether a hundred people watching *Woza Albert* at the Market in 1980 could bring down the state—the answer is "No." But it was one small part of a very large conversation raging across the country.

SC: You mentioned language. Could you say something about the function of dialect itself, apart from the content of a play?

MP: Well, first you have to try to explain a bit more clearly what you mean by a dialect. We have 11 official languages, and each of those languages has a sound and quality of its own. I think of dialect as being various kinds of Englishes ... if that's what you mean by a dialect.

SC: Yes, and language that identifies an individual as part of a particular population.

MP: We use class and race signifiers in our language when we develop plays. Just as one might imagine a member of the Irish working class being portrayed as a clown in certain theaters, so we have certain groups that have become the butt of certain kinds of jokes. It's quite an easy laugh you can get if someone portrays a character from that particular language group or that particular subculture. So we do have all of that raging across our system.

And then we have the language purists. For example, there are people who think that proper, authentic, deep Zulu should be rejuvenated and used in certain kinds of theater. In some fantastical future there should be a festival in every official language. There are many festivals that advance the Afrikaans language. The National Festival in Grahamstown was originally an English language festival. The emerging position is that the languages of plays should be truthful to the condition portrayed and everything is presented in English subtitles.

Malcolm Purkey (April 2011)

SC: I was looking at a clip of So What's New, *your comedy, on YouTube. That was much more difficult for me to understand than, say, the Congolese man in* The Girl in the Yellow Dress.

MP: Sure, absolutely. There are certain plays that play on language and slang in order to make points, and to mark some of the play as being from certain communities, truthful to the slang of the streets. If you went to the theater at the Market from when it was founded, the white audiences were going as sympathetic fellow travelers in a struggle. Part of the generosity was that if I didn't understand everything—"That's life. I'll accept that I can only understand fifty percent of this play in front of me." And one of the games that some of these plays played is to use humor that only the black audiences would understand. The experience in the theater would be that the black audiences were roaring with laughter and the white audiences would be saying, "What was that about? What exactly happened?"

There's another generation who are feeling "I don't have to be that generous. I want to hear this." We've been debating at the Market Theatre whether to use surtitles.

SC: Would you like to?

MP: I'm of the generation that liked that previous, complicated game. We'll have to get into a situation where the next generation are all multi-lingual, or we might move to surtitles.

SC: Malcolm, could you tell me about South African theater as a whole? I'm sure that you're familiar with New York theater and its enormous division between Broadway and the theater that you and I work in—the theater of ideas. Does that same split exist?

MP: We don't have the enormous number of venues or the enormous audience that you have. We certainly have what we could call a *fringe*. We also have 2000-seaters like the Monte Casino Theatre, where we've had every major British and American musical that you can name.

When I started out in my career, in the early '70s, there was a chance to see the latest Pinter, the latest Ayckbourn, etc.... The public theaters, which were then white-only state theaters, would fund them. But increasingly we do not see those kinds of plays staged because the audience has changed radically. A black majority audience doesn't have a taste for that.

SC: The theater they see is real meaningful theater.

MP: Right. The theater that makes the most sense and seems to do the most business is theater that is a mirror of people's lives. In the case of *So What's New*, for example—it's about women who are just interested in running shebeens, and maybe selling some drugs on the side, and are trying to make their way in the informal sector while their daughter is on the street. Those kinds of plays talk directly to our audience.

SC: Are you satisfied with the funding you receive?

MP: The Market Theatre was very complex. It emerged as an independent, free-thinking free theater, but it was highly subsidized by international embassies and what I call *liberal conservative capital*, who were positioning themselves against apartheid. Fortunately it became what is called a *cultural institution* in early 2000, because otherwise it would not have survived. We are one of six formal cultural institutions that the state funds directly. Not the National Arts Council, but the Ministry.

But in their wisdom, the Ministry think that we have to raise our programming money from other sources, and that's where the National Arts Council is supposed to play a part, and the Lottery's supposed to play a part, private donors and embassies are supposed to play a part. That was an ideological decision taken post '94. Up until that point, there were four white apartheid institutions that had too much money. So this was an attempt to spread the program money around. However, it's not really working anymore because the National Arts Council simply doesn't have enough money. We are low on the list, especially because all we want to do is create theater—as opposed to theater for education, theater to advance HIV/AIDS cures, etc.... The people who love the theater as I do— in effect *for itself*—have to make a very special case to find the money.

Judith Malina (February 2012)

"I do theater in order to further politics.
I was trained to that. I was trained to—before
I knew it was political theater."

Judith Malina, one of the most influential stage directors of the 20th century, was also a highly acclaimed actress and playwright. Along with her husband, Julian Beck, she founded the Living Theatre in 1947. She was a committed anarchist and pacifist, and the Living Theatre has reflected her social concerns. Her most noted productions include Paradise Now *and* The Brig. *She's received many honors, including the Ordem de Merito (Brazil), the Lola d'Annunzio Award, the New York Innovative Theater*

Judith Malina (February 2012)

Award and several Obie Awards. She's been inducted into the Off Broadway Hall of Fame and the Theater Hall of Fame. Malina died in 2015.

Steve Capra: *Everyone associates the Living Theatre with shows like* Paradise Now, *from the '60s. Are your audiences different now?*

Judith Malina: Every single audience is different. Every moment is different. Every night is different. Every person is different.

SC: But today's generation today is so different from the generation of the '60s. What do you think of the generation today?

JM: I'm thrilled by the generation today! I think they're much more intelligent, much more active, much more political.

SC: What about the direction your theater's taken since you started?

JM: It changes every night. Every day at 6:00 we have notes and we make changes.

SC: You're based largely in the works of Artaud and Piscator, is that right?

JM: Yes, among thousands of others, but certainly those are important influences. It's based on the history of culture. All art is based on the history of culture. I don't think I'm any different from anybody else in that way.

SC: What would you tell people who are starting out in the theater? What would you like to see them do?

JM: I'd like them to make steps I can't even imagine yet. I'd like them to go further out and explore their own creativity.

SC: What are the biggest problems you've had? Have they been financial, or have they been political?

JM: Only money. I have no problem except money.

SC: It's been more of a problem than politics?

JM: No, politics is no problem. Politics is the work we do.

SC: But you've been imprisoned.

JM: Yes, I've been imprisoned. It's a wonderful step. It's a great experience. It's always brought me forward.

SC: Are we closer to "the glorious, non-violent anarchist revolution" [a phrase Malina often used] than we were when you started?

JM: Every day.

SC: In Korach *[a Living Theatre play by Malina], you show us that Emma Goldman said, "We will lose—"*

JM: "—every battle except the last one."

SC: *Do you really think there'll be a last battle?*
JM: Well, either that or we're going to destroy the species on the planet, yes.

SC: *But won't there always be resistance?*
JM: I hope so.

SC: *I mean resistance to what you're trying to do.*
JM: Resistance to what anybody's trying to do. Resistance is part of a function of humanity. It'll happen all the time. And even when we win the last battle and eliminate prisons, national boundaries, police, armies, government, there'll still be problems. There'll be further resistances. And further progression. And further difficulties. That's part of our glory.

SC: *Which came first for you, the politics or the theater?*
JM: I do theater in order to further politics. I was trained to that. I was trained to—before I knew it was political theater. I was doing political theater when I was eight, nine years old. I was reciting at these big rallies in which my father was engaged with many people who were trying to make the American people and certainly American Jews realize what was happening in Germany. And they didn't realize that. And there were great rallies and there was a whole movement to further this. And as a little child I recited these poems in German about the German Jewish children and my mother would count the handkerchiefs and say, "You only got 30 handkerchiefs tonight! You better make them cry!"

So, I was trained to political theater. I didn't know that was political theater. I thought I was reciting poems.

SC: *You also work in verse. Is your verse theater as political as your other work? I don't think of verse as being political. I think of verse as being elevating and aesthetic.*
JM: How can it be elevating and not be political?

Robert Wilson (August 2013)

"People can respond any way they want.
I myself don't attach too much meaning
or interpretation to things."

Robert Wilson (August 2013)

Robert Wilson is esteemed for innovative staging and design. He's best known for works such as Einstein on the Beach. *He's accomplished as a director of his own and others' scripts, both drama and opera. His many awards and honors include the Dorothy and Lillian Gish Prize, the Olivier Award and five honorary doctorate degrees. He was nominated for a Pulitzer Prize for* CIVIL WarS: a tree is best measured when it is down, *a large five-act musical work which has never been performed as a unit. He's the founder and artistic director of the Watermill Center, an arts laboratory on Long Island.*

Steve Capra: *Your images can be taken in the abstract, as design. In* Time Rocker *you have a time machine that looks like a fish, and characters in cages. Is your audience to resist making denotative associations with them—"That looks like Victorian costume therefore that's the setting; those look like cages therefore people are imprisoned"—or do you want us just to respond emotionally, as if it were expressionism?*

Robert Wilson: People can respond any way they want. I myself don't attach too much meaning or interpretation to things. I don't try to invite too much meaning.

SC: Making certain types of theater, we know exactly what effect we want to have on the audience. Can you tell me what effect you'd like to have?

RW: My theater's something you experience, and to experience something is a way of thinking. So you can see the same performance every night, you could be in the same performance every night, but your experience can be very different. And though you're seeing or you're doing—as much as you can—pretty much the same thing, you can have a different experience. If you have too many fixed ideas about what it is that you're doing then you miss all these other possible ideas and things that can happen. My approach is more of a Zen approach where you can think about a situation in multiple ways There's no fixed interpretation.

SC: Your work slows down time so much. I was introduced to your work at (the installation H.G.) the Clink Street Vaults in London where time stopped. Could you say something about that? Time came to a standstill.

RW: I did it for the anniversary of H.G. Wells' *The Time Machine*, thinking that ... how time becomes space. In a split second everything is there. That's just what I was thinking about.

Robert Wilson (August 2013)

SC: When you were in Portugal, you said the avant-garde means rediscovering the classics. Could you say more about that?

RW: Socrates said the baby is born knowing everything.

I remember years ago when Donald Judd put a hundred mill aluminum tubes in these two army barracks in Marfa, Texas, and people were surprised and they didn't know exactly how to think about it, what to say. I said immediately, "I believe five thousand years from now it'll still be very interesting because it's classic. It's like the pyramids. The lines are classics. The classics are the only thing that ever made it." Now we pretty much agree that it was a great work. People had to rediscover the classics.

And George Balanchine ... his choreography.... I read a review of *The Parties* in the *London Times*. They were probably shocked and surprised. If any choreographer's going to work 500 years from now it'll be George Balanchine because they're classical compositions. He was the Mozart of the 20th century.

Einstein on the Beach—people didn't know what to make of it when Philip Glass and I did it in '76, but it has a classical structure—four acts with a theme and variations. People are beginning to recognize it as perhaps one of the great works of the 20th century. It's a classical piece. So we always have to rediscover the classics. It's a body of knowledge we're born with.

SC: You didn't have a traditional theater education. We think of art as building on art that came before it. How do you do that without a traditional education?

RW: Man is always discerning the same patterns, the same geometry. It's an inherent knowledge within us. I was always fascinated by classical patterns—whether it was a necktie or an arrangement of plants, a building or music. So whatever I did, I was always preoccupied, in this frame of mind. So if I'm arranging this dining room, or redesigning a building, designing an opera—it's all part of the same concern. When a reporter asked him, "Mr. Einstein, can you repeat what you just said?" Einstein said, "There's no need for me to repeat what I just said because it's all the same thought."

Whatever I'm doing is my signature and my signature has always been something that concerns classical patterns.

SC: How do you approach a classic script, such as Peer Gynt?

RW: You have to respect the master but you also have to avoid becoming a slave to it so you find your own way of doing it. I can't rewrite Shakespeare. I wouldn't want to rewrite *Hamlet*. It's probably the greatest play ever written, but I had to find my way into it.

Lee Breuer (April 2014)

> "You put some Nietzsche on one tray,
> you put some Disney on the other,
> and you wait till the two balance."

Lee Breuer was the recipient of a MacArthur Fellowship, a Bunting Fellowship, a Guggenheim Fellowship and two Fulbright Fellowships. His honors also include Obie Awards including one for Distinguished Achievement, the Helen Hayes Award, the Archangel Award at the Edinburgh International Festival and the Chevalier de l'Ordre des Arts et des Lettres from the French Ministry of Culture. He was the co-artistic director of the theater company Mabou Mines, which he co-founded. Breuer died in 2021.

Steve Capra: *I was looking at* The Performing Arts Journal *from 1976. You wrote that you worked "with a lot of doubt, and some fear." Could you say something about that? How does it feel to work now?*

Lee Breuer: Talking about being afraid of working is a way of making yourself attractive. It's gaining sympathy. So I'm not so sure that any of that's real. Right now I work with more anger than fear. I think my anger is realer. You're always afraid because you think you're full of shit. You're afraid you'll look bad. At that point I was afraid of not being loved. So, I think, "Love me. Love me. Love me" is what that article was all about.

I really feel that the ego is so endless, and feeding it is such a total life-long proposition that you just look back at what you used to feed yourself, and you're shocked. "How could I be so uncool? How could I be so stupid? What an asshole!" All of that stuff is just self-advertisement. I was just trying to advertise myself as a sympathetic *avanty-gard-ey* artist in *New York-ey* who just arrived and had a little theater and was very broke and who needed sympathy. I look back at some of the non-fiction writing I've done and I think that's some of the falsest stuff I've ever come up with.

SC: But you starting writing the Animations *[a set of Breuer's puppet plays] at about that time, didn't you?*

LB: I did. The writing, the fiction was straight. I wasn't lying much in the fiction. See, when we started Mabou Mines, we had these kinds of superstars around... Everybody grew up in the '60s generation. Everybody had screwed around Europe for five or ten years. Everybody had been to India and back. Everybody had gone the same ridiculous route.

SC: *Well, it was a productive route. It produced a lot of terrific stuff.*

LB: Right... It was the only culturally ordained route we could have taken.

I read your interview with Judith [Malina; see page 21]. She's a political animal and she's very focused. She's an amazing woman. She's such a Brechtian archetype. She's Mother Courage with the banner. I remember I saw Living Theatre stuff when I was in my 20s and it deeply affected me. And of course I was really playing anarchist and everything else, because we all were. I wasn't so much a political animal that way. I don't quite see art as getting out there and waving a flag and trying to change the world so much as a pilgrimage.

I've always been interested in religion but nothing very specific. I think I'm very interested in the *idea* of religion, without being religious. It's a potpourri, a smorgasbord—a little Indian bullshit here, a little Hindu bullshit there, a little Buddhism there, Christianity over here, some Jewish references here. Just mix it all together and make a pie. Then try to make that pie taste good. I got a little bit too cynical to actually pick a religion and say, "I'm gonna go that route." I got very interested in Mahayana Buddhism for a while and then kind of slept off that one.

SC: *But you're not cynical about your work.*

LB: Sure I am. I'm both really cynical and really a romantic—which is a really strange combination. I can flip from one to another like a cinema edit. Sure, I wanna believe everything's great, everything's gonna be all right and people are good and all that sort of stuff. And then I turn around and people look like pigs and the whole affair looks like... I read this in *The Times*. Some scientist was asked "What's the most powerful force in the universe?" They were expecting him to say, "the strong force that holds nuclei together" or... He said, "Greed." And then he said, "No, not greed. Jealousy."

SC: *That's not very scientific of him.*

LB: I think there's a tremendous force in jealousy for the artist. I think they're skipping around trying to one-up each other. Richard Foreman once just called it a little chess game.

Lee Breuer (April 2014)

SC: *What are your work habits?*
   LB: I used to work best on the subway, late at night just riding around and writing on napkins and stuff. That was lot of fun. Now it's in the bathtub.

SC: *I'll try that.*
   LB: I have very kinky working methods. If it's any good it usually is close to an inspiration. I mean, I get an idea and I gotta get it down. Then when the inspiration is over, I give up. I can't sit down for two or three hours a day and work like Tolstoy. I've been trying to. It doesn't quite work out too well. I can't get focused enough. I can't remember what I thought was important the day before. The key is I need to be emotionally involved when I sit down.

SC: *Would you tell me about your production of* DollHouse *[a radical adaptation of Ibsen's* A Doll's House*]?*
   LB: I had a very talented cast of actors that ranged from 3 feet to 6 feet tall. All the men were little people. All the women were average height or taller. We staged it in a Victorian dollhouse. All the furniture were scaled to fit the men.
   I stole the concept from Brecht. I saw the last version of the [Berliner] Ensemble *Coriolan*. It was a genius work. Coriolanus and Aufidius were the two shortest people on stage. Ekkehard Schall and Hilmar Thate were his two big stars and they were both about [*gesturing*] that tall. He gave them each an army and the armies were all six-foot-six or more, so they had this little general leading the army. Ekkehard looked like Mickey Mouse in *The Sorcerer's Apprentice* because they put him in a glove leather robe. He would do all these Roman poses and the sleeve would flop over. He looked just like one of the Disney's seven dwarfs.
   What I saw was this idea of making the more powerful the shorter, on stage. So in *DollHouse* the patriarchy with the power were the shortest. And the women ... were taller. The maid was the tallest. So there was whole gradation of power that had to do with height in reverse. It was totally clear the instant you saw it. As soon as you saw a rather Victorian pretentious gesture by one of the men—you immediately got the picture.

SC: *I'm interested in what you expect of the audience, what their responsibility is.*
   LB: They don't have one, because theater is what's already in their heads. You see, theater doesn't take place on the stage. Theater takes place [*pointing to his head*] in here. There's a second dialectical whirligig

Lee Breuer (April 2014)

there. What I'm presenting to you on the stage you (the audience) counterpoint with what you presuppose that moment on the stage is supposed to be. If I come somewhat close to what you think—you like it. And if I disagree with what you think, you tend not to like it. That's pretty much what criticism is.

You do make the theater [*pointing to his head*] up here; what's onstage is just my contribution. I'm adding another layer to what you're thinking. I can *change* your head. But my images become only an aspect of what you already know in your head the drama should be.

SC: *Certainly the audience we saw at La MaMa—at* La Divina[1]*—is going to be very different from an audience who has never seen downtown theater, and you address both of them. They must perceive very different things.*

LB: That's democracy. If you have 50 people who your work corroborates it, and 40 people who it doesn't, you're probably gonna have a hit. But if you have 60 people who it's counter to what's already in their head... This is a little bit cynical, but this is the way Broadway works. You wanna make any money, you tell people what they already know. You show people what they wanna see.

SC: *Your work can be accessed on different levels.*

LB: I get a little balance game going. You have a scale and you wanna keep both of the trays off the ground. So you put some Nietzsche on one tray, you put some Disney on the other, and you wait till the two balance. And the Nietzsche isn't valid until the Disney gets off the ground, and then the two of them are valid. It's a little kind of—I don't wanna be pretentious about it—philosophical position, that somehow bullshit can be balanced with truth and then you get something like a super truth ... an *ubertruth—or ubercamp.*

SC: *You draw from all these different forms. How can you be sure it's gonna have unity? What rule do you give yourself to make sure that the whole piece is gonna fit together?*

LB: Let me tell you where that came from. It's a Disney rule. I took my youngest kid down to Disneyworld. There was a Swedish pavilion here and an Icelandic pavilion there and a Japanese pavilion over there.... And they were playing canned music in every one. And every time I would see people walking around, their steps would change when they walked into another musical environment. They would walk out of the

---

1. A mixed-media play by Breuer with wooden puppets, live music, video, and actors, produced a few months before this interview. The main character is a (puppet) dog.

Lee Breuer (April 2014)

Japanese one into the Swedish one and their steps would start changing. It was *brilliant* (in the British sense of the word)! Perfect manipulation. It was life.

The idea in *La Divina* is that when Rose starts listening to her tunes on the radio, every time she switches stations and we hear a different kind of a tune, her life changes. She hears country-western—she has a country-western accent. She listens to a tango station, she speaks with an Argentine accent. She completely changes persona every time the music changes. The environment forces you to become *it*. If you were in the middle of a flood and you walked outdoors, you'd be underwater. Instead of that, you're in a soundscape. Whatever the environment is, it's inundating. It encompasses you. It drowns you. You are swimming in it and it is your environment. It is the world. You change as your music changes. The unity is chaos theory.

SC: La Divina incorporates a lot of your earlier work. It's very much based on The Shaggy Dog Animation.

LB: It was a rewrite of *The Shaggy Dog Animation*. The second part is a rewrite of *Ecco Porco*, and the third is a rewrite of *The Warrior Ant*. It's those three pieces making one unit.

LB: Yeah, along with some of my early work, too. And it's going to include little essays about my work—kind of a *Walk through your life book*—along with performance poems including *La Divina*. Titled: "I don't want to change your mind. I want to change your music."

SC: I understand that you adapt other writers' scripts, but do other directors direct your scripts?

LB: Rarely—There is a group called Rude Mechs [Rude Mechanicals] down in Austin. They did a good version of *B. Beaver Animation*. And right now there's also a version of *Gospel at Colonus* happening in Texas. I kind of divide my work between the adaptations like *DollHouse* and *Gospel at Colonus* and my original work. It's really hard to get anyone interested in the original work because it's very specific to how I direct and how I would stage it.

SC: Which have been more successful on stage?

LB: Depends on who's watching 'em. The most successful commercially was *Gospel at Colonus*. That went to Broadway. Big mistake. That was the worst experience of my life.

SC: Well, you got a Tony nomination for the adaptation, didn't you?

LB: That was an insult. The *white boy* gets a Tony nomination when it's all black music and a young Morgan Freeman and a blind black group that has since won five Grammys—*The Blind Boys of Alabama*—was passed over.

SC: So that was the most well received.

LB: The most well-received *commercially*. It made the most money. And the way it makes money is ... for example—take the Arena [Theater, Washington, DC]. It bounced the black attendance record up the year that we went there. They bring a successful production with a black cast into their repertory, then they can go running off to the National Endowment and say, "Look at our attendance record—subsidize us."

Richard Eyre (September 2014)

> "I don't have any time for people who say,
> 'Oh, you shouldn't mess around with classics.'
> Classics can be messed around with by anybody and
> they're still there. Nobody's taking them away from you."

Sir Richard Eyre has directed in every stage form—Shakespeare, straight drama, musicals and opera. Between 1987 and 1997 he was the director of The National Theatre, London. His other work includes productions at the Royal Opera House and the Metropolitan Opera House. He's the recipient of numerous honors, among them five Olivier Awards including the Olivier Lifetime Achievement Award and three Evening Standard *Awards. He's been appointed Commander of the Order of the British Empire and Member of the Order of the Companions of Honour.*

Steve Capra: *It was interesting last night hearing you mention that you're approaching the opera,*[2] *in terms of rehearsals, the way you would approach a straight play. Could you say more about that? Could you tell me about the differences between directing a straight play and opera?*

Richard Eyre: Well, the first obvious difference is that opera singers come to the first rehearsal knowing the part thoroughly. It's very rare at this level that you're working with singers who've not played the part in

---

2. Eyre had spoken on *The Marriage of Figaro*, which he was directing at the Metropolitan Opera.

Richard Eyre (September 2014)

another production. And that's rare in the theater. In the theater, you're much more likely to have a cast that starts with a clean slate, and you all work together finding out the piece in a collaborative and collegiate way.

What I think I mentioned last night is that, first of all, they're singers and they have this extraordinary gift—a much more quantifiable gift than acting because the judgment of an actor's performance is to some extent quite subjective. Yes, we can all agree that there are some excellent actors, but it's unlikely that we'd agree on who they are. It's much more subjective than the singing voice. It's an athletic skill, to some extent, to be able to sing those big roles.

Part of the job of a director is making a social group cohere so that you have the same sense of values and ambitions and aims and aesthetic—and communicating that sense to the singers. What I do with a play on the first few days of rehearsals is sit round a table and just talk through the play, reading it and talking. With opera rehearsals I do a similar thing. I say, "I don't want you to sing it. I just want you to speak it." And it's sometimes quite hard, because they associate words with music. Saying it will make you concentrate on the meaning. Sometimes, particularly if you know a part well, you can sing and sing and sing, and you're almost on an automatic pilot.

I've found out as a director that it's much better to encourage actors to have a go at something, to talk about a scene, rather than saying, "You're going to do this, you're going to do that." Just seeing how they use the space and how they interact with the other actors before intervening. And the same with opera singers. It is true nowadays that singers are really up for what I'd describe as proper detailed acting work. It's not just stand in the middle of the stage and belt the song out. That's very much a thing of the past.

SC: Could you talk about those differences in terms of blocking and stage picture?

RE: Well, I'm always aware of the stage picture and the whole image. And in opera you've got to be aware of bringing things quite far downstage. In a big house like this you simply can't be properly heard if you go too far upstage. You have to conceive of a stage picture that is quite concentrated towards the front of the stage but doesn't give you the feeling that there's just a line of people across the front of the stage. In that sense it's rather different to staging a play. Most theaters are quite small and there's not that kind of chronic problem with audibility.

By the time I start rehearsing, I have a very clear idea of how I want the stage to look and more or less the kind of mise en scène, the positions of the actors. But, you know, things change in rehearsal and I like to see what the singers come up with. Sometimes things happen and I think, "Oh, I had no idea that was going to happen, or no idea that that could happen at that moment."

SC: Are there rules for dealing with the other differences?
    RE: No, there are no rules. You can mess around with a classic. It's slightly harder to mess around with *The Marriage of Figaro* than, say, Wagner, because *The Marriage of Figaro* is a comedy, and to some extent farce. So you've got to honor that. You can't do a highly conceptualized production of *The Marriage of Figaro*. I don't have any time for people who say, "Oh, you shouldn't mess around with classics." Classics can be messed around with by anybody and they're still there. Nobody's taking them away from you. It never bothers me, the sort of outrage, "Oh, they've destroyed this great masterpiece." Because, you know, next year somebody else'll do it and not destroy it.

SC: You must work closely with your conductor, James Levine. What sort of decisions do you make together?
    RE: We talk about character, really. Most of his notes to the singers are about character and interpretation and text, rather than the mathematics of the music. We talk about interaction between the characters and how to achieve the maximum effect. Sometimes he'll say, "I think that scene or bit of *recitatif* lacks a bit of tension," and I'll say, "Oh, yes, isn't it a bit slow." And then together we'll sort it out.

SC: If we could talk about straight drama... Can we talk about Shakespeare as being a third form, like opera and straight drama?
    RE: Not really. But there aren't that many people in the world who can speak Shakespeare really well, to make it sound absolutely natural and at the same time do justice to the poetry. It's quite hard to teach. It's kind of... it's very, very hard to teach somebody if they don't have an ear to how a line falls, and how the emphasis falls. Sometimes actors really mangle text in order to force a meaning out of a line that the line can't carry, and often it means it gets terribly slow. I find that unbearable because part of the attraction of Shakespeare is the *extraordinary* velocity of thought. If it's slowed down to a sort of pedestrian pace, it just becomes very dull.

SC: You've said that Shakespeare is in the DNA of British theater. Can that last?
    RE: I think it will last, because Shakespeare is still taught in schools.

Richard Eyre (September 2014)

Every theater, almost every theater in the country, at least once a year, will put on a Shakespeare play, so I can't see it fading away. In fact the passion for theater has, if anything, increased over the past few years. People have got less interested in movies and more interested in live entertainment.

SC: My gosh, that's great to hear!

RE: It's a sort of refuge from the internet. More and more people have become bound up in their devices and spend time staring at screens. The corollary of that is that people desire contact, and it's a very vivid form of contact, the theater.

SC: We're accustomed to dividing playwrights into veins. Can we talk about direction styles in the same way?

RE: Not so much in the English-speaking theater. In Germany the idea of *Regietheater*, director's theater, is very current. You will see highly conceptualized productions where an idea—a single, strong idea—is placed on a play, and essentially the play is serving the director's concept. That's quite rare in the English-speaking theater, where the tradition has been, and still is, very much to realize the aims and intentions of the writer.

SC: You've directed musicals as well. You're so well known for your production of Guys and Dolls. *Can musicals reflect life with the same insight, the same intensity as a straight drama?*

RE: Musicals tend to be love stories. So it's a quite narrow area of human experience. And the musical is very much commercially led because they're expensive things to stage. They involve a large number of people and large number of musicians. So, by definition it's expensive, *ergo* it tends to play in a larger theater. So less risk is taken.

I suppose you could make a case for *Book of Mormon* dealing with issues in a way that ... it's a satire and it's probably more pertinent than most straight plays on Broadway. So I would say it is possible. Now there was a very good musical in London a couple of years ago called *London Road*, which was about a small town in Norfolk and a crime that was committed in the town. It was a very profound piece which was all sung. And I don't know if you've seen the show at the Public, *Here Lies Love*, a show about Imelda Marcos and about the fall of Marcos. It's a political piece, but it's very inventively staged and that's wall-to-wall music.

SC: In light of the fact that there are film and television and the internet in the world, can theater regain the importance that it had for Ibsen's audience?

Richard Eyre (September 2014)

RE: I don't think so for a moment. I don't think it has that kind of power to shock. It still has social engagement, but... Ibsen was a great, great genius and by definition geniuses don't come around too often. Ibsen, Chekhov—they're landmarks in world theater. Ibsen was writing when the theater was the only medium apart from the novel. There was no television, there was no, there were no movies. So he had a sort of singularity, a position that couldn't be replicated. I thought *Angels in America* was a very brilliant play, but it didn't sort of move mountains in the way that some of Ibsen's plays did when they were first performed.

SC: *In the book* Talking Theater *you asked David Hare about Peter Hall's thesis that Brechtians will survive over Beckettians. Would you answer that yourself?*

RE: Yes. I would say that a Brechtian... Epic theater is a really vital element of all theater. The ambition to put a little world on stage is what Shakespeare does. He takes the high and low in society and *concertinas* between intimate scenes of personal relationships and public scenes of political relationships—which, you know, Brecht did. And there's a sort of currency introduced by Brecht which is incredibly valuable. I don't think that's gonna die, that kind of appetite for dealing with the world through drama, the collision of the private on the public and vice-versa. I wouldn't nail my colors to either mast; I don't think it's true that either strain in theater will expire. It's propaganda, what David was saying. "These are the plays that I like to write, so I'm saying this to support my polemical position."

Getting back to your question about Shakespeare.... As long as Shakespeare is performed, Shakespeare is the model dramatist, because he does deal with whole worlds, whole societies, in a way that very, very few writers have attempted. So the model is always there in front of us.

The popularity of Beckett is interesting because he's actually become more and more popular year by year. There was a production of *Waiting for Godot* recently in a Broadway theater. That wouldn't have happened twenty years ago. There's a sort of currency for poetic theater. I mean, all theater is metaphor. Everything in a theater is not real. Everything stands for something. So it's a poetic medium. Abstract theater can be very, very potent.

Brecht himself is much less performed, partly because for years the Brecht estate would license only very few translations—and they were so bad, most of the existing translations, like Eric Bentley's translations. Brecht had a currency in the '60s and '70s and then pretty well disappeared from view. But as a model for directors and writers, he's had a much more far-reaching influence than Beckett.

SC: You asked Tony Kushner if theater is uniquely suited to deal with society. Could you answer that for me?

RE: Yes, I think it is, because of what I said about Shakespeare and Brecht putting a world on stage, putting a line of chairs on a stage and saying, "That's a parliament. It stands for a parliament." In *Hamlet*, you get the state of Denmark. Even a poor production of *Hamlet* will give you a sense of a whole political world, and also a whole world of very complex psychological relationships. That is dealing with the world and I think the theater does it particularly well because of that ability to be metaphoric, to be poetic, to be like Shakespeare—to put a world, a society in microcosm in the theater. It's much more effective than film in that regard, because film is so literal. You can't just suggest a world by a piece of furniture in the way that you can in the theater. You have to show everything in film. It's quite a heavy-handed medium.

SC: In Talking Theater, you talk about British theater and American theater as having a real difference between them.

RE: Well, they do. In practice they do. But of course British theater is hugely influenced by American theater. Arthur Miller and Tennessee Williams are still staple diet of British theater. Miller and Williams were writing their plays at a time when British theater was incredibly anemic. So it got a shot in the arm from American theater. The influence still to this day is quite strong of American theater and probably much stronger than the influence of British theater on American.

Anne Bogart (October 2014)

"I try to speak to the highest possible part
of who I am as a director, because I'm the first audience."

Anne Bogart is one of the artistic directors of the SITI Company, in New York, which she co-founded in 1992. Her work focuses on two techniques, Viewpoints and Suzuki. She's the author of three books of essays. She's been awarded three honorary doctoral degrees as well as a Guggenheim Fellowship and a USA Fellowship. She's also received two Obie Awards, the Doris Duke Performing Artist Award, the Association for

Anne Bogart (October 2014)

Theatre in Higher Education Career Achievement Award and several other honors. She's taught extensively and is head of the Direction Concentration at Columbia University School of the Arts.

Steve Capra: *Back in 1983, in* The Drama Review, *you wrote that you were unhappy that theater lacked social and political concern. Do you still feel that way about the theater now?*

    Anne Bogart: I think it's changing. I grew up saying, "Art and politics don't mix." I finally had to say "Why do I say that?" and "Why is it that all the plays are about you and me and our apartment and our problems?" Whereas in Europe and in most of the world, the theater was about people and their relationships, but also the bigger picture. And then I discovered, around that time, that all of our predecessors that I looked up to—people who were involved in the Group Theater and the Living Newspaper etc.—had all, between the years 1949 and '53, either left the country, were blacklisted or changed their tune. And I realized that the most effective political action is one which is forgotten. I grew up not thinking that the theater had anything to do with politics. And then to look back and say, "Oh—isn't that interesting that abstract expressionism was also born during those years." I come from a generation that was encouraged never to think politically in terms of the arts. But I think we're now in a renaissance. A lot of people—playwrights like Tony Kushner and Emily Mann and Suzan-Lori Parks, people like Oskar Eustis—are deeply politically engaged. It's a renaissance of political engagement now. Thank God!

SC: Can the theater become as important as it was to Shaw's audience, to Ibsen's audience? After all, there are film and television in the world.

    AB: The theater was needed in a more profound way when it was the only form of representation of human social interaction. But I do think it's become more important than ever. The smaller the screen of the computer becomes, the more significant the theater is as an unmediated event. It's important in very different ways as a place of encounter. So I'm very optimistic about it.

SC: That's good to hear. You've written that Brecht is your father and that theater at its best is political. But you wrote in your latest book[3] that you don't like didactic theater.

    AB: I said Brecht is my father and Gertrude Stein is my mother, which gives it a kind of paradox of someone who is deeply and politically engaged and Gertrude Stein, who is questionably not.

---

3. *What's the Story: Essays About Art, Theater and Storytelling* (Routledge, 2014).

Anne Bogart (October 2014)

I'll tell you why I don't like didactic theater. The theater is about ambiguity. I think that's why it was originally created by the Greeks in 500 BC—to say, "Okay. Law is important and political action has to have no doubt. But you have to have someplace for ambiguity and doubt to live." And that's where it lives, in the theater, in the great tragedies. Didacticism is saying, "This is the way it is," but that's not what the theater is. The theater sets up oppositions and within family or political discourse or what have you—it's there that we meditate on paradox and ambiguity. That's the essential role of theater. The minute the theater is saying, "This is the way it is," or "Go vote"—if that's the author's message, then I personally don't respond to it as strongly as something that is saying, "Here's two people or two social systems or two families that are in opposition with each other and yet they love each other." It's a much wider field. So you need political conviction, laws, restraint for your social systems but you also need a place for ambiguity. I still don't think that didacticism is particularly interesting.

SC: You've said that you're attracted to theater with terror in it, but yet you've done Chekhov. How do you find terror in such gentle work?

AB: I don't believe those plays are particularly gentle. There is restraint in them but they're powered by massive passions. I think that the characters in Chekhov's work are incredibly selfish. And they're ridiculous! They're clowns! You know… "To Moscow! To Moscow!" Actually, where the three sisters lived was the suburbs of Moscow. It was ridiculous that they couldn't get to where they wanted to go. They're complainers, they're dreamers, they're unable to act. And it sort of showed why the revolution happened. The reason those plays are great is they are connected to deep terror and violence and acuity and humor. I don't think they're nice plays and if you do them nicely they're not that interesting. They need a critical quality.

SC: Well, when you devise a play, you start from your own imagination. That must be very different from approaching a production through Chekhov.

AB: Definitely different. What I start with is not so much imagination but a question. For example, the first devised work I did with my own company, SITI Company, was called *The Medium*. It was 1992. And imagine 1992. There was no internet. There was no email. And yet I thought, "Okay, there's a lot of thinking about what the new technologies are gonna do." So I wanted to make a play about how these new technologies that were winging in our direction would change us as human

Anne Bogart (October 2014)

beings—our relationships, the way we function, the way we live, the way we die. And I wanted to use all this new thinking about what then we called "virtual reality." So that was the central question—"How are these new technologies affecting us?" It wasn't my imagination.

I had to say, "But I need an anchor or a character or something that actually the audience can care about." And eventually came up with Marshall McLuhan, who was like the grand-daddy of thinkers about that. He was talking about television but if you read him now, it's not about television, it's about the world we're living in. He foresaw this current world. So, the devising process is very different because you don't have the genius of a Chekhov.

SC: *In* What's the Story *you point out that we should never talk down to an audience. But most of the audience comes to the theater without any of the wherewithal that you and I do. I would think that they would sometimes need a lot of help in the experience.*

AB: Yeah, help is one thing. I need help when I go to the theater. I need to know how to look at it. I need clues. I need to be told what my job is in the first five minutes of a show. But I won't say to myself in rehearsal "Will Joe Shmoe from Peoria get this?" I want to speak to the highest part of every audience member.

You know, I saw a production years ago. It was the first show Ivo van Hove did at the New York Theater Workshop. The first thing I ever saw of his was this impossible O'Neill play called *More Stately Mansions*. Impossible.

SC: *And enormous.*

AB: Enormous. Five hours long. And impossible. And I remember coming to the theater... It was a preview but it was a full house. The actors walk out on stage, they bow to the audience, they bow to each other, and then all but one of them go to the side of the stage and sit on folding chairs. And the one left, which is Joan MacIntosh, the magnificent Joan MacIntosh, takes a deep breath and at top speed she starts speaking the first eight pages of the play, which is a monologue. Top speed! And I suddenly went "Ha! Oh my God!" And I sat forward, like "If I'm gonna be here I really have to listen!" And as I was listening, in the first 12 minutes of the play, I started hearing that *thump* that happens when people are leaving, the *thump* of the chair going up. He lost a third of the audience. The rest of us stayed for those five hours, had an amazing journey ... but afterwards I had to think about that a lot. Because I thought, "I could never do that to an audience."

Anne Bogart (October 2014)

What we do as Americans—we're a populist culture, democratic—is that we say, "Okay, we're gonna be real easy in the beginning and then We'll *hit 'em hard* in the middle. We'll build to it." He went "No. I'm gonna hit you hard now because if you want to stay here, this is how you have to work. This is how you have to participate." And I thought, "He can do that because he's Dutch and the Dutch have subsidy. They don't care. But I'm an American, we don't have subsidy." I do think the audience needs help, but still in that first five minutes he was telling us how we had to behave as an audience.

I try to speak to the highest possible part of who I am as a director, because I'm the first audience. So that the actors are speaking not to a low belly-laugh level person, but to a part of me that laughs with something that I've had to put together myself. We do need to help the audience, but the question is "Which part of the audience are we speaking to?" I think the theater is a gym for the soul, and I think we go to work out. So, I want to work out. That doesn't mean I don't want to laugh or be inspired or moved, but I want a workout.

SC: You've said you don't appreciate a real stress on style. But working with Suzuki and Viewpoints, aren't you doing that to create a specific style?

AB: Absolutely not! The *worst* of Suzuki and the *worst* of Viewpoints does seem like a style. But it's to mitigate style. It's to move beyond it, to have a more authentic presence. It would be terrible if the Suzuki training were done in a play. The same thing with Viewpoints. To do a Viewpoints improvisation in a play doesn't make sense. But with the Suzuki training, perhaps an actor can be stiller, have their voice come from a lower place. Their legs are strong, they're not shifting back and forth, when they make a gesture it's clear... With the Viewpoints training, maybe it's true that an actor actually has more of a sense of space, they don't wait for a director to tell them where to go, they make a choice based on the composition in the room.

It's as if in a ballet they put the ballet barre into the ballet. That would be not interesting. So this is the ballet barre. It's very frustrating to me because a lot of people study both of those techniques from my company and me and then they go and put it in the plays. But that's not it! You're defeating yourself.

SC: You write so much about neuroscience. How does that translate into the mechanics of the stage?

AB: The study of neuroscience has changed how I understand the way audiences relate to the stage. It's changed everything in terms of how I understand what consciousness is, and awareness, and attention.

For example, in the last 15 years there's been a discovery that neuroscientists call mirror neurons. It's based on the old adage "Monkey see, monkey do." It was discovered first with monkeys, where a neuroscientist came in after lunch to do some work with these monkeys and the monkeys were hooked up to an MRI machine. And he accidentally noticed that when one monkey was picking up a banana to eat it and another monkey was watching him, the exact same synaptical patterns happened in the watcher as in the doer. Not just the synaptical patterns but the muscular activation.

Of course it turns out that mirror neurons exist in humans. So what you suddenly understand in the theater ... what an audience is doing is actually stopping themselves from doing what the actors are doing, muscularly. So if you were an actor on the stage and you just did that gesture that you did, and I'm watching you, I would keep myself from actually imitating you. Because we're imitation machines. So you're actually affecting the audience through your physical gesture. It's amazing!

What I said earlier, that if you have Suzuki training, that when you make a gesture, it's clear... If you make a clear gesture, it affects the audience. If you just do a "kind of, sort of" gesture, it *doesn't* really do anything. So just the fact of what the audience is experiencing, I've learned from studying neuroscience, just as a start, is massive.

SC: *Could you say something about technology in theater?*

AB: I learned this from Thomas Friedman's book *The Lexus and the Olive Tree*. The *Lexus* stands for High-Level Technology Culture. The *Olive Tree* stands for ancient culture. He says that our salvation as human beings is to find a balance between the two. If you go too close to the *Lexus* area, you lose your soul, you become all about technology. So I think of theater that has too much technology, you lose the soul, the meat, the body. But you don't also want to be a Luddite, you don't want to actually say, "technology doesn't exist."

He said, "Where in the world do the lexus and the olive tree balance the most?" The answer is the south of France. You have this beautiful landscape and incredible cooking and then you have the high-speed train that goes right through it. I try in my own theater to create the south of France. If I use hi-tech sound, or hi-tech lighting, I won't have the stage move. If it's all technology or too much video production, I have to say, "Where's the balance? Where am I gonna put the hi-tech and where am I gonna leave it in the olive tree area, where it's the actor's body on the stage?" So I'm more interested in balancing consciously the relationship between ancient culture and new inventions in technology.

SC: *Do people respond to your work, the same production, in the same way around the world?*

AB: Just this week we did *Radio Macbeth* in Tbilisi. We decided not to have supertitles. And they loved the aesthetic experience. I don't think they really understood the play even though it's *Macbeth*.

Some audiences in this country have been so drained by technology that they're not present. That's painful. You know, you always want to get the right audience in—people who come into the right situation and mood.

SC: *People who come carrying the expectations that you want?*

AB: That's a good question. I think audiences need to be prepared to come into the theater. How do you do that? I don't know. I just remember once we did our show *bobrauschenbergamerica* at the Krannert Center in Illinois. I came out afterwards and there was this line of young people standing there and basically they just said, "We want that. Whatever just happened, that's what we need in our lives." That's my favorite audience, where you feel like you're necessary—or *useful*. But if you feel like you're just somebody's entertainment, then it's not so fulfilling.

Julie Taymor (May 2015)

"The main thing is to make sure you love what you're doing, that you're passionate about every project."

Julie Taymor is a director of theater, puppetry, opera and film. She's best known for The Lion King, *for which she won Tony Awards for Best Director, Best Designer and Best Original Musical Score. She's also well known for productions of* Juan Darién: A Carnival Mass, Titus Andronicus *and* The Magic Flute. *She's been given several Drama Desk Awards. Her many other honors include a MacArthur Foundation Fellowship, a Guggenheim Fellowship and the Hewes Award for Concept Puppetry and Masks.*

Julie Taymor (May 2015)

Steve Capra: *In 2003 you gave a very interesting interview to Michael Kantor. You were talking about* Lion King *and you said, "You have to give an audience what they didn't know they wanted." Could you say more about that? Because certainly that's risky, artistically.*

Julie Taymor: Yes, but to me it's creating something that's fresh, expanding people's minds, transforming their experience and transforming their hearts and their intellect. If you give people what they want, which is what is the commercial *raison d'être*—"Wow, we gotta give them what they want"—then you haven't changed anything and nothing can grow.

If you followed anything from that *Lion King* story... I did an experiment with three different versions of how I could do the characters—with make-up like *Cats*, or half-mask, or the big head, double-event thing. I said, "Look, I'm gonna do three versions of five characters as an experiment," because there were a couple of people who had doubts about whether you could do this and have the audience be able to look at the human and the animal simultaneously. When we did them, they all worked, but clearly the first idea—which was the one that's been in there for the last 18 years—was the most interesting. And Michael Eisner said, "Let's go with your first instinct. The bigger the risk, the bigger the pay-off."

And I think that it has followed suit. *Lion King* is the most successful entertainment in all venues in the history of the world—not just Broadway, not just theater. We have 10 or 11 around the world every night. It still feels *now*. Every country makes it their own, but there is a common bond between every country in the experience of *Lion King*. We were allowed to be inventive. And I think people were really taken to some new place for themselves. I was very lucky to have a major company like Disney support it all the way—that's so rare!

I love to take risks and for the most part they work. But some things don't work, and they don't work for various reasons. The most important thing is that you have collaborators—other artists, actors and producers—all with you on the same boat, going to the same place. Meaning "Okay, we're gonna take this risk, but we're gonna take the risk and we're gonna go there all the way." And that's tricky, to find those collaborators.

SC: I'm interested in the relationship between the avant-garde and Broadway, the mainstream. Because sometimes it seems like they're in two unrelated theater worlds.

JT: Well, *Lion King* is *avant-garde*. When you say, "Broadway," it

Julie Taymor (May 2015)

conjures up certain things to people. And when you say *avant-garde* you can't conjure up anything because it's *before*. We all see it as something ahead of its time, and Broadway is so expensive that people are really reluctant to take gambles like that.

So, it's hard to do it both in one. I don't want to talk a lot about *Spider-Man* because of course it was a dark moment, but I will say quite frankly, I loved what we were doing. We just didn't get to finish it. And it was very *avant-garde*. It couldn't fit within the rules of even how you do a Broadway show. It was its own beast. The story is a phenomenal story, but we just didn't... We didn't get it there right, we didn't finish it. And people lost their nerve. People blog and they're ready to talk about things before things are done. But it's like cooking a soufflé. You cannot open the oven before it's ready. You may want to, but if you do, it may fall.

SC: To speak of Grounded[4]—*I'm interested in the way one-character shows work. They don't work through dramatic action, for the most part. They don't work through character interaction. What is it that keeps the audience so engrossed?*

JT: When I read the play, the story is very visual, what she's describing. It's the most difficult thing for a director when a one-woman show is written where it really is like a radio show, where you can imagine her in the drone station. She says it's in a trailer, there's air-conditioning, there's the Barcalounger.... It's all described. You have to be very careful not to be redundant with the imagery. And so in this particular production, very different from other ones, the visualization is an exteriorization of the interior landscape. It's not literal. It's a metaphorical and also symbolic way of using imagery. Its point is to enhance the audience's experience, not be redundant with what the actress is saying.

In some cases, we had to cut some lines from the text, with the approval of the playwright. He was there the whole time. Sometimes he would say, "Well you're doing that, so I don't need to say this." And I'd say, "Precisely."

SC: You mentioned that the playwright was present. Can you talk about the stages of rehearsal? Certainly they must have been different for Grounded *than for* Lion King.

JT: Well, I got asked to do *Grounded* in November. I think they weren't even sure they were going to do it this year. I read it one night,

---

4. *Grounded*, by George Brant, was currently playing at the Public Theater, directed by Taymor. Its sole cast member was Annie Hathaway.

Julie Taymor (May 2015)

said "Yes" the next day. Annie was already on it—Anne Hathaway—so I felt it'd behoove me to take myself out to L.A. to meet her. Because I've never done a play where I'm the second person hired.

So we talked about it. The ending of *Grounded* is not the same. What you saw is not what's in the original text. I had an idea for it. And it took some time for the writer to take that in. Because *Grounded* is very successful. It's been done many places, it's won awards. And both Annie and myself, and Oskar Eustis, we all felt that you could try another ending. It's very valid for a new play to have different endings. Shakespeare—people changed the endings all the time.

SC: That's the fun of a new play.

JT: It is! So, thank God, he was open to it, and wrote a new ending. Then I immersed myself in the imageries inspired by the text. I collect huge amounts of visuals and pick my team. Elliot's always my team, pretty much—Elliot Goldenthal, who is a composer I've worked with for thirty years. He did the soundscapes and score. And I worked with new lighting projections and set designers. Never worked with any of them and I adored them. They were recommended by the Public and I thought, "Good opportunity! I can go from a massively huge production to a one-woman show."

SC: That must be great fun!

JT: It is! And also, being with Annie, who's fabulous to work with, for six, seven hours a day for four or five weeks in rehearsal room, one week of tech. We were ready!

You know, when you do a big show like *The Lion King* or any of the other big things I've done—*Juan Darien, Green Bird, Spider-Man*—they take a lot more tech. This was extremely easy compared to doing those things because the forces are small. And that's a pleasure. Though I feel that it's fully visualized. I don't feel there's anything else I would want. It's not a heavy tech show.

After we opened that, two days later I went to Mexico to do the last week of rehearsals on *Lion King* in Mexico. You're there with 200 people so it's just like … *crazy*! And when you do *The Magic Flute* at the Met [the Metropolitan Opera]—which I've done—every two years they bring it up—they have 200 people backstage at The Met. That's just the way that they have there.

So… I met her, I got with my designers… And then we did four weeks of rehearsal and did it. So that's a process. It didn't take a lot of time.

Julie Taymor (May 2015)

SC: As opposed to Lion King, *which was workshopped.*

JT: Two years. You would spend a minimum of two years on a new musical that has to be written and has to be designed. You can't really do it in a year. But Shakespeare, you'd spend probably a year in prep. I think I spent a year in prep on *Midsummer Night's Dream*. We did workshops with children. I wanted to see what the fairy world would be. So I did experiments—and it was fantastic!

SC: If you could talk about your work with world theater... Could you say something about what you have to do to translate between cultures? You've said that the mask techniques of Lion King *were redesigned, reconceived from the original techniques.*

JT: Techniques are up for grabs. Like the technique of a shadow puppet, anybody can do that. That's not stealing culture. Everybody gets inspired by techniques. You use an oil lamp, then the oil lamp becomes a light bulb, then somebody from a foreign culture says, "I like the oil lamp better." You use a modern technique of fire, you use leather, you use plastic, paper... That's not important. What I don't do... When you read reviews and they say, "Oh, she has Indonesian Wayang Kulit and Bunraku from Japan." It's as if I took Bunraku... It takes eighty years to become a master Bunraku performer. And there are no women doing it! I don't do Bunraku! Having a person manipulate a puppet in full view, that is inspired by a technique I saw in Japan called Bunraku where you see the manipulators. But in Bunraku, they're all in black, and there's three of them. So I would never say that I'm doing anybody else's theater.

The Lion King—The costumes are a complete blend that end up being my own design. Because you get inspired by techniques and images and then hopefully it goes through you, does its business in your heart and your mind and comes out in a personal, individual way that makes it original again. The costume of Scar is definitely inspired by Japanese costumes, but it's not Japanese.

There are two or three masks in there... When I finally got exhausted on the 400th mask I just said, "Oh, do that African mask." But the rest of them—all the lead characters—are my design based on Disney's designs, but they look more like my work than Disney now because my aesthetic is different. Even the poster of *Lion King*—that was my concept because I didn't want the air-brushed look of Disney. So I said I'd like it to look like a Japanese wood block, like wood block print. So somebody took my mask design and did a black woodcut design of

Mufasa and I suggested that color of saffron, which is such a strong color. So that's very not-Disney looking.

Wayang Kulit is also something that I would never do. *Wayang Kulit* is the leather shadow puppets that have traditions in the *Mahabharata*, in the *Ramayana*, and there's a way of carving them and painting them and then manipulating them. I'm not a puppeteer, I've never done that. So, do I make leather shadow puppets? I have, but they're not Javanese. It's just materials.

It's like Balinese painting, with the terraced rice fields. They didn't paint oils or tempera before the Dutch came, but you wouldn't call them Dutch paintings. They learned how to paint from the Dutch. All they learned was how to use oil paint or tempura and canvas or wood. They were inspired by Dutch painters but their *way of painting* is Balinese.

SC: *You said in 2003, "Broadway is a good measure of a cross section of an audience and whether it can really appeal." Do you mean that Broadway audiences are representative of the population?*

JT: I do think that *Lion King* has a cross-section of all types. Because it has very non-traditional theater techniques and world theater techniques in it. To me Lebo M's music, South African music in three different languages, four different languages, is *refreshing*. It's not American. It's something else.

SC: *In light of the fact that there are television and film in the world, can theater ever get back the position that it had for Ibsen or Shaw in terms of social influence?*

JT: Probably not. Unless it becomes a more of a crossover. I really truly believe that theater can be filmed well if it deserves to be. Not every theater piece translates to that, that well. But, for instance, eventually Annie may make a movie of *Grounded*, I don't know. This production would actually shoot very well for a television audience. It's just we're not there yet with the unions, with the cost. You could say because of the way Netflix and Amazon and all this is going, there is room for event screening—what the Met does when it takes its operas and puts them out on live HD in movie theaters. There's an entire audience across the world now going to opera that only has to pay $20—as opposed to $250.

So, the beauty of theater is that it's poetic, that it's not naturalistic. That is one of its virtues. There should be a way to blend, to crossover more. I think it is the future. It's beginning in England. We haven't really figured out how to do that here. People are worried that it will take the place of live theater—I don't think so.

John Doyle (August 2016)

SC: *You've talked about the importance of spectacle. Do you think that filming of the live event will lend itself more to being free with spectacle?*

JT: Well, I think it allows people to see things that are not about realism. The audience has to be able to see on TV, or in an event screening situation, something that's still stylized. If they accept it in a theater they should be able to accept it on a TV or movie screen. But you will never replace a live event with cinema or television. Never!

Immersive theater is coming back in a major way, where people like to go in and move around. I think the proscenium house is a bit of a dead form, the classic theaters on Broadway. I would like to have much more alternative spaces used.

There are ways to experience live theater that's more dimensional. Even in *Lion King*, just the coming down the aisles makes it more 3-D than 3-D. I was trying to do that with *Spider-Man*. If you were up in the balconies and you had people flying and landing next to you, it was an extraordinary circus experience. People love that because you can't get that in movies. And you can't get it on television. So, theater does have to recognize that what it does well it should do more of and not try and be just a postage stamp picture that you could put on a television.

SC: *Could you give some advice to new directors who are just starting to work?*

JT: Well, there's tons of advice. The main thing is to make sure you love what you're doing, that you're passionate about every project. You have to believe in it, love it, and want to spend the time. They're not stepping stones to the next thing. They in and of themselves have to be really where your heart and brain go.

And it's great to challenge yourself. I might do a TV show of a certain kind that I've never done before because that could be "Wow! I've never tried that! I'll try that! Do I have the skills? I don't know." Traveling is the most important thing, stepping outside of your culture and being in a place that's not so comfortable, out of your comfort zone.

John Doyle (August 2016)

"We've not killed the theater yet
and I don't think we will."

John Doyle (August 2016)

John Doyle has been most applauded for his direction of Sweeney Todd, *for which he was given a Tony Award, a Drama Desk Award and an Outer Critics Circle Award. His several other awards include a Drama Desk Award for his direction of* The Color Purple, *two Lucille Lortel Awards and a Special Citation from the New York Drama Critics Circle. He's served as artistic director of four UK theaters and between 2016 and 2022 he was the artistic director of the Classic Stage Company in New York.*

Steve Capra: *You're so well known for paring down works and working minimalistically. What principles do you use?*

John Doyle: You know, I've never called myself a minimalist. One reads that about oneself, but I never think of myself as that, really. I just start in the room with the actors. I do have a sense of how do we get to the essence of the story without being reliant on technology or physical hardware. I come from a background in the UK of theater-making that was usually made without enormous resources, without a lot of money, and so that trained me into a way of working that was not dependent on things that really are better used in the movies. I'm really interested in how does the human being tell the story.

If you take something like *The Color Purple*.... *The Color Purple* sits on a set which I also designed. But we don't need the set. All you really need are the 17 actors and the 15 chairs that they use, and a couple of baskets and a sheet or two. But that's it. You could put it all in the back of a truck and go anywhere in the world and do it, and not need anything other than the people and those things. And that's where I start, with almost everything I do. You look at everything from a very clear, simple point of view, putting the story first.

What I felt with *The Color Purple* was that—I felt that the material deserved a production that honored Alice Walker's novel. If you read the novel, it's very simple—few characters, very much inside a girl's head, her relationship with God, her relationship with her lost sister. I wanted to bring that out in the feel, the fabric of how you feel when you watch the show.

With something like *Peer Gynt*... *Peer Gynt* is such a massive, potentially massive extravaganza...

SC: A five-hour play!

JD: Yeah! And you've got to stop and look at where you are in the world and think, "Well, nobody's gonna sit through that anyway. Forget it!" The audience's concentration span has got shorter. The 90-minute

John Doyle (August 2016)

play is normal. Television, I suppose, has done that to us. It's redefined how much we can cope with at a time. I'm not saying you *shouldn't* do the five-and-a-half hour *Peer Gynt*, but if you read some of *Peer Gynt*, it's unstageable. Some of it, you think, "Well really, this man is talking to the sphinx. How are you going to stage that?" I felt that what the piece said, what Ibsen was getting at, about man and his ego and how the ego can start as the imagination and end up as an embittered, out-of-proportion part of mankind, which is Peer's journey…. He has to go back home to find out who he really was. I felt in this day and age more than any other time that's worth saying. You know, in Trump's America, that's worth saying.

But I also knew that I was doing it in a space where I didn't have the resource to have a lot of stuff. So I wanted the relationship between the actors themselves to be what told the story. But I heightened that by being in the round, because when you're in the round you can't have stuff. Otherwise someone's not going to see. The round in a way by its very nature denudes the work and already strips the work away.

So I don't think I ever go into the room with one point of view about how to simplify it. But that's what I always come out with at the other end. I'm interested in the actor and the words more than anything else.

SC: You didn't take that approach, as I understand it, with your production of Passion. Theatermania [a theater website] called it "large and lush."

JD: Well, actually the set was not all that big. I also designed that. It had a floor, it had mirrors on the back wall. It was an illusion, really. It wasn't particularly large. It was only a cast of ten, a small orchestra and it was in the same space as you saw[5]—it was in Classic Stage. Probably richer than some of the work people would expect of me, but not if you compare it to a lot of stuff that you would see today, no. It's still very simple.

SC: Can you give me some principles for directing a musical as opposed to directing a straight drama?

JD: No, I don't think there's any difference. Now, it's helpful, if you're directing a musical, if you are musical. And of course there are things in musicals that are techniques, like how a song builds, how you physically use the stage in relationship to the build of the music, how the lights crudely get brighter as the song goes on because the song lifts up.

---

5. The space in which the author saw Doyle's production of *Peer Gynt*.

John Doyle (August 2016)

There are simple techniques that you learn by being musical. And fortunately, I was given the opportunity to be musical when I was young.

But in terms of the approach with the actor, I don't believe it is—and I don't believe it should be—any different. Or at least not the kind of musicals that I want to do. There are some musicals that are very ... slick, where ten dancing girls come on and they all look the same. It doesn't interest me in the least, because to me that's not about humanity. So, I will ask the same questions of an actor, or work in the same way, in the musical theater rehearsal room as I would do in a straight play.

Inevitably, the scenes are shorter, because the song takes the place of the scene. The song is like a soliloquy in Shakespeare. The song says the thing that the actor can't say by speaking. The song is the verse of the play, if you like, of the musical.

There are certain things that you need to gradually know about, but, you know, when I started directing musicals, nobody had ever done a course on how to direct a musical, or wrote a book about it. I learned on the job. I learned from doing it—what works with an audience, what doesn't. You have to listen. You have to listen, of course, to the music. You have to listen to the actors, *always*, regardless of whether it's a musical or a play. It's your job, to listen to what the actor's saying, feeling, understanding. At the same time, musicals have more—not always in my work—but they can have more applause points than a play. An audience in a musical is given the opportunity to show its approval.

SC: Do British audiences respond to theater in the same way that Americans do? Would they be as engrossed in The Color Purple?

JD: Oh, they'll be just as engrossed. Will they be so overt in their need to show that? Possibly not. You know, one of the things that I find slightly annoying here as a theater audience is that every, *every* audience has to stand up at the end. I'm only interested in standing up if I truly believe that I'm seeing something the likes of which I've never seen before. I just think it's become generalized. It's become the thing to do, to be seen to stand up. I don't think people *shouldn't* stand up if they love something, but it should be a unique experience. But, you know, in terms of enjoyment, in terms of respect for the work, I think the audiences are the same.

There are certain things I don't like in American theater. One—it never starts on time. It drives me crazy! You know, you go to any show in America, it starts seven or eight minutes late. In Britain, you start at the

John Doyle (August 2016)

time that's advertised, or you don't get in—simple. We should do that to our audiences again. We should train our audiences to be respectful.

Audiences in both countries, although it is possibly a little bit worse here, are disrespectful to the actors by the amount that they are looking at their technology through the evening, or taking photographs, or looking at their phones. I find that deeply, deeply disrespectful. But equally, nothing excites me more than going and seeing an audience full of people of all ages, which you certainly see here. And I'm always amazed that people do go to the theater as much as they do in New York City because it's so darned expensive.

SC: Is it easier to work in Britain in terms of the whole production process, in terms of the business? Theater is healthier in the U.K. than it is in this country.

JD: I don't know that I agree. There are a number of issues in there. One—in the U.K. some theater, what you call not-for-profit theaters—I don't like that term, because that suggests that profit is the only [*laughing*] healthy thing to have—if you take that element in Britain, it's subsidized, so they get subsidy by the government. And so they should. And that should happen here, too—right?—much more than it does. To me, if a country is going to be truly civilized, it should provide health, it should provide education, it should provide arts. And probably many other things as well.

So, some British theaters—of which there are fewer and fewer—are fortunate because they can take greater risks because the government is funding the risk. In terms of rigor, however, in terms of people working hard, studying hard and exploring deeply, I would say, if anything, there's more rigor here than there is in the U.K. I'm only thinking of the Broadway shows you know. It's no fun doing eight shows a week on Broadway. It's hard work. They work hard and they are disciplined and they keep it together beautifully and it's beautifully looked after. Because there's a greater investment in the work in this country, financially, than there is in the work in Britain. People get paid much less money in Britain to make theater. And less money's put into it in the first place.

Now, everything I'm saying is a generalization, obviously. But I would say that the work ethic is as good if not better here than anywhere else I know in the world.

There may be at the root of what you're bringing up an element of lack of confidence, oddly enough—oddly, considering this country exudes so much confidence in so many ways. Because in the English language, the theater has always been perceived to have been a British

John Doyle (August 2016)

product. But I think that's changing. You have more new writers than we have now, probably. And certainly if we take a musical as an example, you created the musical theater. We didn't. All right, we birthed William Shakespeare and the Jacobeans and many others, but not all of them. I mean, we didn't birth Chekhov or Ibsen or so many others.

But, of course, with companies like the Royal Shakespeare Company and the Royal National Theatre, we have given out some of the great actors of the world, with great training. But I think that's changing. You've given out many of the great movie actors of the world. And many of those people are coming back into doing theater. So there's movement all the time.

I would say one is no better or stronger than the other.

SC: Do you put any weight on what the critics write?

JD: I totally respect the critics. I don't have any sense that there shouldn't be any criticism or anything like that. Not at all! But I don't personally read them too much. Somebody said to me, "You should read *The Color Purple* reviews," and I read a few of them and they were really great. But a lot of the time I don't. It might be difficult now that I'm artistic director here at Classic Stage. It might be different because I may feel that I *have to read* what is said because of the work being done in the building.

But if a critic said, "John Doyle shouldn't be doing this. He should be doing that," it wouldn't make any difference to me. I wouldn't listen to that. I mean, why would I? That person doesn't know me. I'm not telling them what to do. And I think the critic's job should be to encourage people to go to the theater. That doesn't mean to say they have to like everything. I totally respect that. Sometimes the things they don't like, you think, "Oh, that's good. I'm glad you didn't like that because I think that's what I wanted you to feel."

I'm not very good at listening to the audience, really, at any level. I just do the work and hope that I'm being as truthful to the story as I can be. My job is to not please but to respect the playwright. That's why I exist, to respect the writer. That's what I care about. I don't want to see a production get bad reviews because that will mean that somebody's going to lose some money somewhere along the line. I don't want to see that happen. But if that is the case, then so be it. The unfortunate thing is that if you read too much of it then the ones that you remember as an artist are the bad ones. They're always the ones you remember. So it's safer, in a way, not to get too involved in all of that.

SC: In light of the fact that there are film and television in the world, can theater ever regain the importance that it had for Ibsen's audience?

JD: Yes. As long as it doesn't try to be film and television. I think the gift that, particularly the movies... Let's keep television out of the framework a little bit because so much of television now is questionable. Not the news part of it and not the documentary part of it. You can watch great sport. But great plays on the television really don't happen anymore.

But the movies, which are such a wonderful story-telling medium, they've made us have to re-address how we make theater. And we have to get back to being theatrical, to being... to doing what *The Color Purple* does.

What you're watching on *The Color Purple*, with people taking chairs off the back wall, making a prison out of those chairs or making a train out of those chairs or whatever they do, you couldn't do that. It would look stupid in a movie. You'd have to have the real prison. Because most—not all, but most movie-making has encouraged naturalism and reality. What theater can do is not encourage naturalism but encourage the abstract, encourage expressionism, encourage a size of... I don't mean an *over-the-topness*, but a stature of story-telling that is immediate and is not necessarily something that can be done on a screen.

As long as the theater can re-address *how* it makes work happen and *doesn't* fall into the trap of using so much technology that it makes movies on stage, then the world's our oyster.

We've not killed the theater yet and I don't think we will, to be honest. I don't think we will kill the theater. It's up to the story-teller, however, people like me, to make sure that we are telling stories that are important. That doesn't mean to say they can't be funny or joyous or light-hearted or anything else. But at every story's core, you have to know why you're telling the story. And it should have an impact on humanity. It should have something to say if it's going to be worth telling. As long as we do that, as long as we keep addressing "Okay, what are we trying to say? How are we saying it? Who are we affecting? How do we develop the audiences by doing that work?," we will live on, I'm sure.

Ping Chong (May 2018)

"I object to the term 'cultural appropriation'
as a negative, because you can't stop that. It happens.
Human beings are always mixing and trading."

Ping Chong (May 2018)

Ping Chong is best known for work that expresses an intense concern with identity and culture using a wide range of interdisciplinary, experimental techniques. One of his best known works, Undesirable Elements, *is an oral history project in which members of the community speak on stage about their personal experiences. Nearly 50 similar pieces have been presented internationally. He's received many honors including the National Medal of the Arts, the Doris Duke Performing Artists Award, a Guggenheim Fellowship and a USA Artist Fellowship.*

Steve Capra: *You say on your website that all your work has been very innovative—and clearly it has been. Is being innovative for its own sake important?*

Ping Chong: I don't think of it in those terms, really. I think of it in terms of being a contemporary artist and speaking in a contemporary voice. The innovation comes out of that need more than innovation for its own sake. It's coming out of a contemporary sensibility.

When I started out in 1972, only the dance world and the visual arts world were using media. Theater was rather stodgy in terms of their relationship to the twentieth and twenty-first century. It was mostly kind of a nineteenth-century paradigm. And I didn't come out of that. I came out of a contemporary construct, in terms of my interest both in visual arts and in film. Those were really my key interests.

Even though my family came from the Chinese opera, I myself came out of visual arts and film, the Chinese opera being part of my legacy. And being someone who didn't come from a Western background, I had to find my own voice. So the innovation comes out of the fact that I'm not coming from a Western tradition. So how do I find my voice? By necessity, that was going to be innovation.

SC: When you directed La Clemenza di Tito, *the* Washington Post *made it sound like that was a traditional production.*

PC: Well, that was a college production. That was what the school wanted to do. It was a gig. That would not be a norm for me.

SC: Right.

PC: I mean, I do things that are out of my own context. Sometimes people ask me to do things that are not what I normally do, and that would be an example. Like, I directed Benjamin Britten's *Curlew River*, a one-act opera, for the Spoleto Festival. That's not my norm. I'm not known as an opera director. Because I come from a contemporary

Ping Chong (May 2018)

sensibility, I welcome the challenge of doing that. A contemporary sensibility is open to anything.

SC: So that's atypical for you.

PC: That's atypical for me, but not in terms of working in a musical theater context—not musical theater in the Broadway sense, but music and theater. Because I started out in life as a performer with Meredith Monk, who's very music-oriented and movement-oriented, so I did have an appreciation of kinesthetics and music, not to mention that I come from an opera family. And in my own body of work there have been a couple of musical theater works.

SC: You just mentioned media. You said once, "Today, theater without media is almost unimaginable."

PC: And I said that a long time ago!

SC: Right!

PC: And when I said it, very few theaters were using media. It was only our downtown crowd that was using media. I started out in '72, and immediately I was using media. For my very first production that was independent of Meredith Monk, in '72, there was film, there was slide projection, there was puppetry. So right from the start I was interdisciplinary and I was using media.

I made that statement about media at the very beginning of my career really. And look at it now! And people who don't know what they're doing with media are using media. I think it's not always used sensitively, although there's a lot of great media designers. When I started out, I think there were maybe three media designers. There were very few.

SC: So we really have left behind Artaud and Peter Brook.

PC: I don't know. Peter Brook I think of as a contemporary artist. He comes from a European tradition, but he was an explorer in his own way. He also made film, as well, but he wasn't interested in media so much. He was a man of the theater first, whereas I was a man of film. I graduated as a filmmaker and a visual artist, so I'm coming from a different place than he was.

SC: You work in so many different forms. Your process must be different for the various forms.

PC: Yes and no. Today the academy describes improvisation to create work "devised theater." But devised theater was going on way before this and had not been termed "devised theater." When I started out, everything I did was devised theater. I'm not saying that I'm the first to do devised theater. It was something that was established a long time ago that they kind of rediscovered at this point and coined it "devised theater." It's kind of a hot item in the academy these days. Everybody's doing devised theater in the academy. I don't know how successful it is outside of the Academy but for some reason it's caught on.

SC: *If you could talk about* Undesirable Elements. *You've said that language is basic to it. When I saw Generation NYZ, I could see the importance of the Spanish, but it didn't seem to me that it was elemental to the concept.*

PC: Well, the original *Undesirable Elements*, the very first *Undesirable Elements*, we used multiple languages in it, but it was primarily in English.

SC: *That must have been great.*

PC: From the very beginning of my career, I used multiple languages in my work. All of that to frame the fact that English is not the only language that exists in the world. Certainly in America today, we're living in a multicultural society, so I've always acknowledged language in other cultures. The use of Spanish is because the person's roots are in Spanish, so naturally that would be used.

SC: Undesirable Elements *is a sort of actualism. Are you making a statement about aesthetic distance? I was that taught aesthetic distance is important to make the audience think about what's going on.*

PC: It's not about distancing at all. It's coming from direct experience. It's coming from an older tradition of story-telling, which is the roots of theater. But it's also theater as activism. These are not actors—these are the real people, and what happened to them happened to them. It's not an actor intervening in their stories. *Undesirable Elements is* both an artistic construct and an act of art as activism. *That's* what's different. That's where it's coming from, a very different idea.

SC: Undesirable Elements *is a sort of civic engagement, civic commentary—*
PC: Yes. Absolutely.

SC: *And you've performed it all over the world.*
PC: Yes.

SC: *Have you ever felt that you're being censored?*
PC: I've never had that experience. The only time I ever had a problem, really, was in a production of the original *Undesirable*

Ping Chong (May 2018)

Elements—maybe I should say the classic *Undesirable Elements*. The original ones always had people from different cultures. And I did one production in Atlanta where I had a Bosnian Serb in the show. It was all teenagers. And someone came up to me after the show and said, "You had a Bosnian Serb"—they're Eastern Orthodox—"You had a Bosnian Serb in the show. You could have had a Muslim in the show, too." But if you saw the show—the Bosnian Serb lived through part of the civil war in the former Yugoslavian Republic. She was at that time, maybe seven, eight. And she says in the show, "I don't hate anybody." The man who said that I didn't have Muslims in the show couldn't see that the point of the show isn't having equal representation of everybody. The point is that we all have to learn to live together.

I understand where he was coming from. I regret that I was upset at the time with him. I would be different with him today.

And then another time I had a young black actor come up to me and say...—in the original show, I had, among other people, a Filipino and a Japanese, telling their own life stories—and I had a black gal in the cast who was half Jewish and half black, who was abandoned at birth and who was adopted six months later by a Mennonite family. After the show, the young black actor came to me and said, "You had two Asians in the show. You could have had a *real* black person." And this completely floored me because—*one*—it showed her ignorance of Asians. She was conflating the fact that I was Asian and that those two were Asians—and so we were all from the same thing. And we were not *at all* from the same thing. That's one thing. And—*two*—she was being a bigot because she didn't see the black cast members as black enough. She's not seen as Jewish, or half–Jewish, or half anything. If she went down South, she would be treated like a black person. And yet this black girl said I needed to have a *real* black person in the cast—which is ridiculous.

So, those were the two moments where I had some push-back.

SC: Even abroad?

PC: I don't recall having any problems from abroad. No.

The idea of *Undesirable Elements* is that this is a microcosm of people who are in your community, the audience's community. And yet there is a parallel existence rather than an integrated experience between the larger society and these other people. The idea of *Undesirable Elements* is that it's a place in which that bridge can be crossed. It's an opportunity to meet members of your community that you don't have any knowledge of—*one*; and—*two*, that you see as *other*. In a way, this project, at least in the United States, is about who determines who is an American. It's like "Why are you more American than me?"

SC: You draw from a lot of different cultural influences. There are people who would say that that's cultural appropriation, and they would say that it's wrong.

PC: I object to the term "cultural appropriation" as a negative, because you can't stop that. It happens. Human beings are always mixing and trading. Hip hop is all over the world. That's cultural appropriation. You can't stop it.

I think that a lot of this contemporary censoring that's going on left and right is ridiculous, personally. I have a real problem with that, because as I say, cultural appropriation is about people's curiosity. People have always been exchanging information. That's human nature. I don't see how you can stop it. I understand the issue of the majority culture taking from the minority culture and not acknowledging the source. That's where the problem comes up. But at the same time, there's just not much you can do about appropriation. The Chinese are wearing Western suits in China—the head of government. They're not wearing Chinese clothes. So where do we draw the line?

SC: To build on that just a bit—you've said that you're "an American artist; the irony is that now we're ghettoizing ourselves by choice." Can you say a bit more about that?

PC: I don't know what context that was said in.

SC: That was in a book called The Art of the Theater: Then and Now. *The quote is "I'm an American artist. The irony is that now we're ghettoizing ourselves by choice. I understand that this act is an affirmation of one's identity. That's important. But we cannot loose sight of the fact that we all live in a society where we have to coexist and exchange ideas and influences with one another."*

PC: Well, that goes back to the cultural appropriation thing. I'm—quote, unquote—Chinese-American, right? But I'm American. If I go to China, I'd be seen as an American, because I don't walk like them, for example. I don't speak the majority Chinese that they speak there, which is Mandarin.

I personally don't want to narrow what I'm permitted to do as an artist. Because, as I say, I'm an American artist. That means that every culture in this country is part of my culture. I don't want to be narrowing myself down to being an Asian-American artist. I don't object to being called an Asian-American artist, but I see myself really as being an American artist because my work spans all kinds of cultures. Why shouldn't it? We're all mongrels here.

SC: In light of the fact that there are movies and television in the world, can theater ever be as important to society as it was for Shaw's audience, for Chekhov's audience?

PC: No. I don't think so. But it is the most human experience still, because it's a direct experience of human beings without the intervention of anything else. It may not have the reach—it can't have the reach of cinema or even radio, if you want, but it is valuable as a direct human experience. I don't think there's much value in comparing those things, in terms of numbers, because it's a different experience. It's as different as eating apples or eating steak. It's one of the riches of our human experience. It's not a competition.

SC: Finally—if you have any advice for young directors.

PC: Find another profession! [*laughing*] It's difficult!

André Bishop (September 2018)

"We are living in a golden age of American theater— and a golden age of American playwriting."

André Bishop was appointed artistic director of Lincoln Center Theater in 1992 and producing artistic director in 2013. He had previously been the artistic director at Playwrights Horizons. He has produced over 80 Broadway shows. His many awards include the Margo Jones Award, the Lucille Lortel Award for Outstanding Body of Work, a Special Award from the Drama Desk, 17 Tony Awards for Best Production and three Pulitzer Prizes. In 2012 he was inducted into the Theater Hall of Fame and he's a member of the American Academy of Arts and Sciences.

Steve Capra: *First of all, Congratulations on* My Fair Lady!6

André Bishop: Thank you.

SC: What's the relationship of the type of theater you do—the masthead theater of New York—to, for example, La MaMa, and the experimental theater, the black box theater.

---

6. Bishop's production of it was running at the time.

André Bishop (September 2018)

AB: Well, I'm not that aware of what La MaMa does anymore. I was very aware of what it was doing in the '60s and '70s. When I first came to New York in '70, I had friends who directed there and worked there and all that stuff. I think in New York there's room for all kinds of theaters, and it would be irresponsible to assume that this building at Lincoln Center would devolve into some experimental theater. That would be what's called *suicide*.

But that said, we did build this third theater on the roof [of the Claire Tow Theater], which is 100 seats, which is *only* devoted to the work of new young writers, directors, and designers, and has a different audience than our membership audience here in the Mitzi and in the Beaumont[7]—or on Broadway. I won't go so far as to say that LCT3 is like experimental black box, but it certainly has a lot of young and edgier writers. The idea was always that we would be able to develop a generation—or two or three—of new, talented people who would then begin working in our other spaces. The point of this third theater on the roof was not just to do new plays. It was to see people and eventually get them working in the other two spaces as well. So some well known—I guess I'll use the word "older"—writer or director would not direct in the third theater. The runs are shorter and the tickets are thirty and twenty dollars.

SC: *So you really include the whole range of types of theater.*

AB: Yes, very much so. We do a wide variety. If you have the occasional hugely successful show like *My Fair Lady*, people who don't normally go to theater on a regular basis, or who just read about you or whatever, assume 250 shows or something.... Only five of them have been classic old musicals—and about thirty of them have been new musicals. Last year we had this very successful play on called *Oslo*, and everyone thought, "Well, all they do is these political plays." And then there was a year we did two Shakespeare plays and everyone said, "Oh, all they do is Shakespeare." And the fact is, we do a wide variety of stuff.

SC: *Does it make much of a difference that Lincoln Center Theater is a not-for-profit theater? It must give you a freedom that commercial producers don't have. Or is the burden of fund-raising so great that it's not an advantage?*

AB: No, no, it gives a huge freedom. I mean, the freedom is that I, as the artistic director, get to pick the plays that I want to do and the

---

7. The Mitzi E. Newhouse and Vivian Beaumont theaters.

André Bishop (September 2018)

artists that I want to work with. I don't have to worry "Will this be popular or not? Will we make money off this play or not?" I never think about things like that.

SC: That's great!

AB: So that's enormously freeing. But the difficult years, the years where either there's a funding shortfall, or when the markets went down—there are all those worries. Some foundations, because of the world we are now living in, are cutting way back in funding artistic programs in favor of other needy things like social justice and poverty and disease.

But, yes, there is artistic freedom—that's for sure. All the plays we're doing this year, when I look at them, my instinct is "They're all good plays. Hopefully, we'll do them well." I don't see that any of them will be a particularly a big money-making event. But that's not what these non-profit theaters are here for. If we judge our excellence and our worth and our success just by the money we make at the box office, I'm outta here. I don't want to do that. I've never had to do that. And it still is a struggle. Here, it's on a very lofty scale, but juggling all the balls in the air of this very big theater at Lincoln Center—which is an extremely expensive place to work—is tough.

SC: You've said that you choose material to please your own tastes. That's great!

AB: Yes, I do, and I always have. In the world that has, again, changed in the past few years, there are people who no longer find that an acceptable *mantra* for an artistic director to have. They think one's own taste is only part of the equation, but one should do this kind of play and that kind of play and use the theater to address all the joys and sorrows of the world. Well, most good plays do that anyway. We all have personal taste. I don't know what it is—it's *non-objective*. It has to do with everything that's inside of us, that informs us. And presumably as you get older and the world changes, you *change*. The kinds of plays I loved thirty years ago I'm not so interested in now.

People say, "What is producing? What is being an artistic director?" And I say, "It's not that complicated. It is the intelligent exercise of your own taste. And hopefully what you like, other people might respond to as well." That's what makes all the variety that we have going on in New York and in this country so interesting. We all should be different. We all should have different axes to grind and different points of view. That's what I feel very, very strongly.

André Bishop (September 2018)

SC: Once you've chosen the material and the director, what is your role?

AB: The key to it is trust. If you choose to do a play and if you hire a director, and if you are involved in the casting, which I am—the callbacks, and I don't go to all auditions but I go to final auditions—the set design I look at. Ultimately, I don't hover. There are producers who do hover. I don't. I feel we have engaged the artistic talents of all these people. We have used our best judgment in terms of matching a play with a director, with an actor, with a designer, and with an *audience*. And now I go away and I have to let them do their work and trust that the can do their work. I don't go to a lot of rehearsals, unless there's a problem. I go to the first day of rehearsal. I go to the reading of the play—it's sort of a tradition that everyone does. I go to a run-through just before they move into the theater and start doing tech rehearsals. And then I go to the dress rehearsal. And I go to the first preview and then I go to every fourth preview. I don't see it every night because what I have is a fresh pair of eyes. Just as the director and the author are getting kind of worn down, I'm still fresh.

But the key to *that* is also to make sure that I, as the producer, and the author if it's a new play, and the director are all on the same page when we go into rehearsal. In other words, that I don't think the play should be blue and the author thinks it's red and the director wants to make it green. We've all got to think it's blue or green or whatever we choose. So that I'm coming in seeing the world of the play the way *they* have chosen to do it, as opposed to the way *I* want it to be done.

SC: You just decide that very early, when you choose—

AB: Yeah! And then you just let it go. You never know in the theater. Someone who you think could be brilliant in the leading role is having personal problems and … you just never know. But if you hover and artistically micromanage—I don't believe in that at all. I want to walk away from it feeling secure that the work that needs to be done is being done.

SC: If we can talk for a moment about world theater and how American theater fits into it. Is there such a thing as a national theater in the sense of style? English theater as opposed to American theater? French theater?

AB: Well, there are clichés that one could say—and I don't know how true these things are anymore. The *mantra*—forever—is that the British theater is more technically based. British actors are more vocally trained. American actors are more naturalistic. British actors are kind of from the outside in. American actors are from the inside out. Then

André Bishop (September 2018)

there's the theory that British plays are not personal—they're social. American plays are more personal and family and emotional. And the French theater, I think, is thought of as being more academic and cerebral—I don't mean the classics but modern writing. I think that's all dissolving now.

So, yes, I do think British theater is a little more technical and American theater is a little more emotional, maybe. That has to do with training. But, I think, less and less so. England has a healthy theater culture because it's a much smaller country. And even though they're cutting back and cutting back, it still is massively subsidized by the government. There's a larger banner to wave because the government is choosing to help wave it. That is not the case in this country at all. Every year you think, "Oh, the NEA is gonna close." Hopefully It'll never happen, but the NEA is woefully underfunded.

SC: If you had a word of advice for theater producers trying to set up companies and to make do with what they have, what would you say to them?

AB: Well, it's changed a lot. When I started at Playwrights Horizons in the mid–1970s, all of us who were starting companies wanted to build permanent institutions. We wanted buildings of our own. We wanted *permanence*. Now the world in general, and a lot of theater companies in particular, are much more *peripatetic*. They come together and do a show when they're ready. Some of the companies that I greatly admire don't necessarily have the overhead an institution has.

My word of advice to someone starting would be "Learn from your predecessors." Because when I began, again, there were hardly any role models—The Public Theater and La MaMa, American Place Theater and one or two others around the country—but that was it. I came in at the beginning of the flowering of the non-profit institution. We were making it up as we went along. You can't do that now because you have too many role models to follow. When I was at Playwrights we had no press agent, we had no management. I didn't go to Yale Drama School in administration.

My word of advice is "If you want to start a company, start a company and build it into the kind of company you want. Build it into where your aesthetic lies, where your artistic soul resides."

I don't mean to be high-toned about this at all. The thing I don't like about the theater today—and maybe this has always been true

André Bishop (September 2018)

since the Greeks—is that young people, because they're young, can be quite intolerant of other aesthetics. We have a Directors Lab here. About a hundred directors come for three weeks and they take classes and they put on scenes and they go to plays and they hear people give talks. It used to be New York, then it became the country, now it's global. And we had a hundred directors this past July from 31 countries—and some really rather dicey countries. I always talk to them, you know, in the beginning. And my thing is that the best thing about this Directors Lab is being with 99 other people whom you probably have never met, from different countries, many with different aesthetics as to what they believe in or look for or want to try to do in the theater. I always say to them, "All I care about is that you are open and respectful to hearing what they say." You can be someone who only likes avant-garde work, you can be someone who only likes Broadway musicals—whatever it is. But being open to someone else's aesthetic does not diminish your own. In fact, it helps define your own, if you really pay attention.

So I feel very strongly that an artistic openness is needed—even if you have very strict ideals and ideas of what you want to do or what you have to bring to the table that is the theater. And it's exciting! I was in, maybe, the second generation of non-profit theaters in New York, the first being The Public and La MaMa and American Place and one or two others. Playwrights Horizons, Manhattan Theater Club, the now defunct Circle Rep, EST, were the second generation. Then there was the third generation. And now we're about the fifth generation—Ars Nova and Club Thumb and, you know, downtown theater. And I find it unbelievably exciting. And when I go around the country, there are hundreds of theaters and many of them are really excellent. The hunger for new work, which was not there at all in the mid–1970s, is vast. We are living in a golden age of American theater—and a golden age of American playwriting.

We're all so insecure, in some way, that we can't pause and say, "Look at what we've done!" But the theater in this country has done a lot. I wish people outside, and those of us who work inside, would recognize that. I don't mean being smug about it—just being proud of it. It was not clear 50 years ago that there would be a flourishing of the theater in America—leaving the Broadway theater as its own island.

Some of these theaters have gone out of business, but everything goes—the dry cleaner goes out of business. God did not come down from heaven and say, "You must start an institution and then it will last forever." Institutions run out of steam, or they run out of leaders who provide the energy, or whatever. But there are all these theaters that've been around for years. It's astounding!

Bartlett Sher (January 2019)

> *"The question of taking risks has to do with your preparation and your impulses about a particular text and where you want to push that text at the time you're working on it. Money only influences the amount of time you have to make it any good."*

Bartlett Sher has been resident director of Lincoln Center Theater since 2008. Prior to that he was artistic director at the Hartford Stage and the Intiman Theatre (Seattle), and company director at the Guthrie Theater (Minneapolis). He's been praised for his direction of musicals, straight modern dramas, Shakespeare and opera. He's been recognized with two Drama Desk Awards, two Outer Critics Circle Awards, a Lucille Lortell Award, an Obie Award and a Tony Award for his direction of South Pacific.

Steve Capra: *A couple of years ago, you said to New York Theater Guide that you're essentially political with a small "p." Can you say what that means? Is all theater political? What does it mean to be political but not to be overtly political?*

Bartlett Sher: Yeah. I mean, every piece of literature, text, event, reflects some political values, ideas, structure or information. So, you know, the most middle-class Neil Simon play has politics in it. It represents the politics of a certain group of people, in a certain time—a certain everything. A Shakespeare—who was essentially a royalist—represents the politics of his time, very specifically. So imbedded in every single text is the moment and the time and the world around it. So you can't ignore—and you have to be willing to explore—the politics and import of everything you're working on. You can't pretend it's separate from that. Even if it's Verdi and it's *Rigoletto*—and it's somewhere else—it's based on a certain politics for the period. And whether those politics have immediate significance now must be asked whenever you do the piece. It's always been important to me that I do that. Now, I say

Bartlett Sher (January 2019)

"small 'P' " because I don't mean to have a capital 'P.' I'm not *espousing* a political point of view. I'm not pushing a political agenda of some kind. I'm exploring what's in the piece itself—in the dynamics of the piece.

SC: Is that why you put the tag on the ending of My Fair Lady?[8]

BS: I put the tag on the ending of *My Fair Lady* to continue the conversation that Shaw began in 1911. In 1911 he was exploring what it meant, the ending, and didn't come up with a satisfactory answer—even for himself. So we asked the question about what the ending meant now and we answered it for us now in 2018.

SC: Would Shaw have approved?

BS: How can we answer that? I don't know that. But I do know that he certainly would have expected any artist to ask the question of themselves.

SC: When you directed Fiddler *and* Oslo, *were you making a statement about Israel?*

BS: *Fiddler*—no. In neither case was I making a statement about a particular political country. In the case of *Fiddler*, we were talking about refugees and about a particular thing—but nothing about Israel. I have no particular agenda about Israel that I'm interested in pursuing. In the case of *Oslo*, Israel is a participant in a political situation which is part of that show. So we had to know about and understand the politics of that region.

SC: You said of Trump, "I don't want to give him the benefit of doing some play about him."

BS: Yes, correct.

SC: So all theater has political content, but you don't want to approach the Trump administration.

BS: Why should we name them specifically? That doesn't mean it's not political. I mean, you could easily say that doing something like *To Kill a Mockingbird* right now in 2018 is a direct response to the Trump administration—but we don't have to talk about them specifically. I worked with Pedro Almodovar on *A Woman on the Verge*. He very rarely gave us notes but at one point in the script the name of Franco appeared. And he had grown up his whole life fighting Franco. And he said, "The one thing we never do is mention Franco," and he made sure we cut it. We do not give them the respect or the understanding of talking about them.

---

8. Sher's production was running at the time of this interview.

Bartlett Sher (January 2019)

So I think there's plenty of ways of dealing with Trump and whatever he's up to without having to give him the benefit of talking about him the way he wants everybody to talk about him all the time. There are many, many ways that we can do it. I think *Mockingbird*'s a very important piece and I'm very proud of having done it when we did it because I think it's a direct conversation with what's going on in our country right now—without having to name or even remotely discuss the current leadership.

SC: Speaking of Mockingbird, *I'm interested in the way you overcame people's expectations. Was changing the structure of the piece, of the narrative, part of your mechanism for dealing with the fact that people had really strong expectations.*

BS: No—I do not have any idea about that. That was a choice that Aaron made for his own purposes when it came to the writing. I don't think that was necessarily a motivation. I couldn't speak to his motivations for doing so. He felt it was important for telling that story in a theater to structure it in a way where we could go back and forth in time—so we did.

SC: I'm interested in the relationship between Broadway or the West End and the type of theater that I've done—La MaMa and the Living Theatre. Because sometimes it seems like they're in two different worlds.

BS: Well, certainly, they are, unquestionably. Yeah.

SC: Is that healthy?

BS: I don't think there's any reason to suggest they should be in the same world. Once the commercial enters into a world, once it becomes a commercial event, which is, in a sense, having to create a certain amount of commercial property. You're working in a different social and political context. So I don't think there is a need to compare them. They both are wonderful. They both can be as wonderful or as bad as anything else.

SC: If we can talk about the mechanics of theater.
BS: Sure.

SC: The New York Times *said that you're known for exhaustive preproduction preparation. What does that consist of?*

BS: Well, if you take a piece like *My Fair Lady,* one has to learn everything about the context of 1911 and the circumstances in which Shaw was writing, and the world of that piece before beginning the work you need to do to set off into your own interpretation. So that work is a preconscious fill-up-your-intuition about a period before embarking on

Bartlett Sher (January 2019)

your own interpretation. So if I'm doing *Rigoletto*, I have to study four or five different versions. I have to look very carefully at what Verdi was interested in. I have to study as precisely as I can other productions of *Rigoletto* and know the environment in which Verdi was writing before I begin to decide what sort of interpretation I'm going to embark on. That's just to make me prepared.

SC: To Kill a Mockingbird *and* My Fair Lady *were so different. Are there principles that people should know about approaching different types of scripts—or do you approach them in the same way, with the same mechanics, and let them speak for themselves?*

BS: That's a false comparison that you just made. One is a pre-existing text which I am interpreting—meaning *My Fair Lady*. I cannot change it, I can't rewrite it, I can't necessarily work on it. The other we're taking from scratch and making brand new, meaning we have the writer there and we're building our adaptation as we go. Those processes require different development processes and different everything. The basic function of my interpretation of a pre-existing text of any kind is essentially the same. *But* when you have a writer there and you can change the text itself, you're in a different world, in a different set of rules and considerations. So in the case of something like *Mockingbird*, it was three or four years of workshops and development—and then even in the course—even in the course of previews, making changes to the text itself as we were developing the piece.

That is not something that's gonna happen with *My Fair Lady* because Lerner and Loewe are not available to rewrite the music or rewrite the text. We're shaping something—or in the case of a Shakespeare—we're doing purely interpretive work.

It's important to make a distinction between the interpretive artist and the creative artist. The interpretive artist is what a director does with a pre-existing reality, a score or what have you—like a conductor—whereas a creative artist—Adam Guettel, David Yasbeck, Aaron Sorkin—could be anyone—they are writing a new piece and their function is very different than my function as an interpretive artist. So when I'm working on new piece, you're kind of melding the two functions.

SC: You said once that theater is more difficult than opera or musicals because the actors are at the edge of the diving board by themselves. They have to build the rhythm. They have to build the layers and build the story with pure language.

BS: Yes.

Bartlett Sher (January 2019)

SC: Can you say more about that? How do you provide the support that they would have with the music in an opera or a musical?

BS: Well, that's part of the job of rehearsal. Rehearsal is, in the case of a play, it's getting inside the rhetoric and the music of a text. It's getting inside the layers of the text and realizing all of it is going to be built on performance—not on some musical idea that comes underneath it with 80 people in the pit. That's rehearsal and that's attention to language, attention to rhythm in language, attention to rhythm in movement. So when you're staging a play and you've worked on a musical or an opera, you find you're suddenly missing one major element. I started working in plays so I didn't realize that until I'd been working in musicals and operas long enough to go "Oh, my Gosh!" When I actually go back to plays, it's so much more demanding because it requires of the actors to invent and develop essentially their own score to support the work they're doing.

Now, you may build that in with a sound person—where you add the music in between scenes or you add music underneath things. That's possible. But you still have to invent that. You don't get that provided to you where you're looking at exactly where Verdi is changing the tempos or doing an *accelerando* or whatever he might be doing that helps you understand where he wants the emphasis to go. You have to make all those decisions on your own.

Now, it's a little easier in Shakespeare because you have verse and you have changes in the way the language is structured to help you understand the rhythm differently based on the rules of prose-versus-poetry-versus-what-have-you. So those thing are scored in there to some degree—but you have to have the knowledge to understand how to unlock that.

SC: Speaking of opera—the Times *reported that you had four days of rehearsal for* Barber of Seville.

BS: No, that's not—I didn't have four days. I had two-and-a-half weeks.

SC: Okay, but still ... compared to a few months for To Kill a Mockingbird. *How do you make the production individual and unique?*

BS: You work fast. [*laughing*] I mean, the thing people need to understand—opera's an extremely expensive art form with large numbers of people involved, and with singers coming from all over the world to participate in it. So, you're not gonna get the same sort of resources. So rather than worry, and rather than say, "I need more

Bartlett Sher (January 2019)

time," you just have to figure out how you're gonna work within the time you get.

SC: I don't know what the Intiman Theatre was like, but because the work at Lincoln Center and at the Met is so expensive, do you feel more constrained? Do you feel like you can't take risks?

BS: No, not at all. No, I think—if anything—no matter what happens—the question of taking risks has nothing to do with money. The question of taking risks has to do with your preparation and your impulses about a particular text and where you want to push that text at the time you're working on it. Money only influences the amount of time you have to make it any good. [*laughing*] That's what it affects! And of course, you're in certain cultural circumstances, you know, in which there are a lot of expectations of the money people pay and what they come to see—and all that is all within a Broadway or a Metropolitan Opera audience situation. But those should be challenged as well, and those risks should not affect an artist's impulse or instinct to take a risk.

SC: You've said that you enter into the activity of searching for an answer. And you said once that you saw The King and I *two hundred times. Does that process of looking for an answer continue after the show is up and rehearsals are over?*

BS: No, usually—I would have seen *The King and I* at least fifty times before it opened, just because I'm in the process of shaping it. But that's because it's an ongoing, active interaction with the text and with this thing you've created and you're constantly shaping it. It's never pinned down and fixed. It's constantly in motion. One of the reasons for seeing it so many times—we had many different people play the king so you'd have to come in and respond to new people who are in it or new actors who are in it. Right now, tonight, we have two different people—Danny Burstein and Christian Dante White—going into *My Fair Lady*. I have to come back and watch their performance and respond to their performance. I do not build a thing and then put them into the slot exactly. I have to respond to that artist and what they are bringing to the piece within the rules and the way I see how it fits within the work we've created. So I think it's more of a *verb* than a *noun*. In other words, this is an active exploration of a work. I could go and see *King and I*—it's gonna be in Japan in July, and I will look at it probably in a very different way when I'm sitting in Japan watching it with Ken Watanabe and Kelli O'Hara than I would be when I saw it in London or when here at the Vivian Beaumont. It's constantly in process and I have to bring fresh eyes to it every time I see it.

SC: I have a final question. In light of the fact that there are film and television in the world, can theater regain the importance that it had for Shaw's audience, for Ibsen's audience?

BS: I think, again, that's somewhat of a false question. Obviously in 1911 there were no such things as film and television. For the consciousness of that audience there was no competition. Their entertainment options were—you know—music halls or plays or pantos or what-have-you. I don't think—I think theater in relationship to television and film has sustained its position in our cultural life. Many, many people still have a very profound interest in being in a room with other people and spending, certainly, decent amounts of money to come and see live theater. And that has not seemed to ebb at all in the current world of—you know—advanced technologies and film and television and Netflix and Amazon Prime and watching things on your phone.

People are still substantially feeling whatever core need they have to come into a theater and experience it and be there. And I think that up to now, unlike, perhaps, music or what-have-you, there are still a lot of ways in which people find it a very important part of their way of experiencing stories that are important to them, or entertaining to them, or whatever function they have for theater in their lives. And I think it's a very strong feeling.

Li Ning (February 2019)

> "There are only two requirements for the government. The first is no nudity. The second is that the contents can't be about the political, sensitive events, like the June fourth, 1989, event in Tiananmen Square."

Li Ning is the celebrated founder and artistic director of the Chinese theater company Physical Guerrillas. The company performs in Beijing, Shanghai and Hong Kong and tours internationally with an agenda addressing social issues. He's also an internationally recognized choreographer and filmmaker. His many honors include the Best Innovation Award from the Shenzhen Dramatists Association, the Beijing Fringe Festival Best Cross-border Experiment Award and a Gold Medal from the Netherlands Done Foundation. At the time of the interview, Ning's production, The Dictionary of Soul, *was playing in New York at La MaMa.*

Li Ning (February 2019)

Steve Capra: *You've worked all over the world. Is your work received differently in different parts of the world?*

Li Ning: I used to imagine that my work would be welcome in Western countries. However, when we did something in a Western country, we found that there were a lot of humorous parts that Western people couldn't really understand—they couldn't really accept them. Similarly, when I was watching Western movies, [*laughing*] I couldn't really get the humor—even in those really good, fascinating Oscar-winning movies. Then I started to wonder if I should shorten the gap—just do something really Chinese. Or should it be more international?

So there were two possibilities. The first choice was to do something that, whether you were Western or of an Oriental background, everyone can understand. Like this production, *The Dictionary of Soul*.[9] The second choice was to focus on the Chinese context—jokes or the reality of their lives—to focus on the Chinese audience. But later I thought that the first audience is myself. I should first feel very strongly about it, then I can do the other things.

SC: So you work to please yourself now.

LN: At first, yes, it was a lot about pleasing himself, but now I want to be more open to the audience, to the culture, to the world.

SC: The audiences at La MaMa loved The Dictionary of Soul. *But many American audiences would find it difficult. How about the Chinese audience? Is it suitable for the general Chinese audience or do you have a specialized audience the way La MaMa does?*

LN: In China, actually, it is very difficult for the audience to accept. The expectation of the Chinese audience—they always want to see a show about happiness, really fancy, with good lights and music. Everything's very expensive. You feel [*laughing*] "Yes, this ticket's worth it!" Everybody's like "Bring harmony together, have a family get-together. We're so happy." They're expecting all of that.

Even my mother couldn't really understand me! For twenty years I've been doing these things, and there are maybe only three or four pieces she can slightly understand. The people who really love it and accept it are mainly people who studied theater abroad, people who are doing academic theater in school, and also young audiences.

---

9. At the time of the interview, Ning's production, *The Dictionary of Soul*, was playing in New York at La MaMa.

Li Ning (February 2019)

SC: Are there other theaters doing the same sort of thing? Is there a healthy avant-garde, the way there is here in New York?

LN: Other theaters have still been doing the old plays, but in these past twenty years, there has been some change in the theater. More *avant-garde* pieces were brought into the theaters. In America, you have this very official, and very organized *avant-garde* space for these shows to be performed—like La MaMa. But recently, these past two years, things are getting better and better in China.

SC: I'm very interested in your relationship with the government. You said that you were critical of the government when you began but you're not now—is that correct?

LN: I want to work with them unless I would feel disgusted about working with them. If I were to feel uncomfortable, then I'd just quit. If the government asks me to do something, I would do it unless it's very like—you know—*co-operation*, or something really—I don't know—*disgusting*.

My goal working with the government actually would be to get my show performed at festivals. The year before last, and last year, we did like two festivals in China. By working with the government we can use the factories and the space. Then we can really gather those young groups and perform in those festivals.

SC: When you say, "working with the government"—what does that mean? Funded by the government? With their permission?

LN: We need permission from the government about the land use. So then we can really *use* that factory, that space. We can decorate and we can make the space into what we want. And second, you do need the money from the government, so that's also the reason. So, actually, it's both.

SC: That would be my next question. You need government funding. But you also charge money for tickets. Can anyone afford to see theater in China?

LN: Half of the ticket price is paid by the government so the audiences pay for the other half.

SC: That's just like here for non-profit theater. But when you started working, did you get in trouble with the government? Have you ever been arrested?

LN: [*Laughing. Ling needed no interpretation for this question.*] Permission from the government for these performances is actually to their credit because the leaders of every province, every city, want people to admire them—like they really did something great. Like "This art festival, we did it! This sports—like the Olympic Games—we did it!" That's what the government wants. They actually don't understand what they are doing—but they don't care, at the same time!

There are only two requirements for the government. The first is no nudity. The second is that the contents can't be about the political, sensitive events, like the June fourth 1989 event in Tiananmen Square.

SC: You can't openly criticize the government.

LN: No, that's the line, there.

SC: In light of the fact that there are film and television in the word, can theater ever be as important as it was in the nineteenth century? Can theater ever be that influential?

LN: It's a very severe problem in China, actually. It's like here. In China old people are obsessed by television shows—even just advertisements about medicine, about hospitals. And the young people are obsessed by video games, computers, YouTube.

SC: Just like here!

LN: But at the same time the theater festivals in China also attract a lot of people. It's more about illusion. The government creates those illusions to let people feel "Oh yes, we are living in a really great time"— the illusion that people are living in a really glorious time.

SC: Are they influenced by what the theater tells them?

LN: They're still dominated by the idea of entertainment at the theater.

SC: If we can talk about The Dictionary of Soul. *What was the rehearsal process?*

LN: I was shocked by the place where my wife was working—with those concrete bricks. I thought, "Oh, this is very interesting." I felt that those things are like art pieces. Then I started gathering more people who were interested in the piece—then I started work on it. I cast a lot of people from all over the country and we lived together—we rehearsed together. We created a lot of like sections—little pieces—there were hundreds of pieces we wanted to put in the final performance. Actually the final performance only used two of them and combined them into this big piece you just saw.

One is like you are a zombie-like body. The other is like you are very energetic. The contrast of these two can be really obvious. You don't have to explain a lot. That's the point of the piece.

SC: *And did much of it come from the actors, or did you explain what you wanted?*

LN: We actually influenced each other. Every performer has his own idea, from his own method of training. Nobody is dominant.

SC: *You've said that you like actors who do things besides act. Did you choose professional actors who are well trained and experienced for this piece, or did you choose ordinary people?*

LN: I prefer untrained people for this production—but I will *make* them into professional performers according to my concept. A lot of the work in *The Dictionary of Soul* is from their true lives. A lot of people were working in factories for a really long time, so they used material from their background. So my job mainly was just to emphasize it—to make it become what it naturally is.

Gabino Rodríguez (February 2019)

"Things are not exactly what they are in the theater.
Things are like they are but also another thing.
If there's a sword on stage, it's a sword
but also it's a piece of cardboard."

Gabino Rodríguez founded the collective Lagartijas Tiradas al Sol in 2003 in Mexico. His work has been presented across Mexico and internationally at the Festwochen in Vienna, Schaubühne in Berlin, Paris Autumn Festival, the Kunstenfestivaldesarts in Brussels, Santiago a mil in Chile, TransAmériques in Montreal and Theater Spektakel in Zurich, among many other festivals. In 2018 he won particular praise praised for his production Tijuana, *which explores the life of the exploited worker.*

Steve Capra: *Gabino, I wanted to talk with you about* Tijuana.[10] *You worked in Tijuana and then you adapted your experience into a play.*

Gabino Rodríguez: Sort of. *Tijuana* a was part of a bigger project called *Democracy in Mexico (1965–2015)*. In 1965, There was a man that wrote a book that was called *Democracy in Mexico*. And he made a kind of an X-ray about how democracy was in Mexico in 1965—about what

---

10. Rodriguez created the production *Tijuana*, directed it, and performed in it.

Gabino Rodríguez (February 2019)

achievements we had made in Mexico after the revolution of 1910 and what exactly was the situation. In that year, Mexico was in a very safe, positive moment economically—like there was growth and so on—but there was just one political party. There was no democracy. There was no opposition; the Congress was one party. So this guy wrote this book. And he had a very optimistic panorama of how democracy will start working and the country will be even better because we will have economic growth and freedoms, like in any liberal democracy.

Fifty years after the publication of this book, we started this project to make 32 pieces—one for each state—about how democracy was doing 50 years after he wrote this book. Now we have different political parties; the Congress is divided. We wanted to explore one aspect of democracy in each project, depending on the region, and to take an artistic approach. We didn't want to make it, say, amateur sociology or amateur political science. Our concern was an artistic concern. But the starting point was the reality—the moment that Mexico was living then politically.

And so I made this project about Tijuana. The project is about one person that goes to a village and changes his identity to be *undercover*. He spends six months working with the minimum wage in order to see what that means, if it's possible to live with that amount of money, or if that law obliges you to work outside the law, maybe in the informal economy, whatever...

So *Tijuana* is a theater piece about a man who goes to a village and works for six months and then comes back and creates the piece. But it's not that I made the thing itself. The piece is presented as a documentary, but I didn't go to Tijuana to work. There's something about how art engages social problems—the artist goes to a place and then lives like that for a little amount of time and then he has an art work that goes to another economy, the art economy. You know the Marxist term, *surplus value*. The surplus in art when art engages with real people is very high for the artist. Artists make a lot more money from what they take from some places. That makes sense, no?

SC: *Yes!*

GR: So, for me it was very important to make a fiction about it and to try to present the person who says, "I will live like you in order to understand." It's living six months without money that makes you understand.

SC: *But did you live for six months in Tijuana?*
GR: No, no.

Gabino Rodríguez (February 2019)

SC: Isn't that interesting! The Los Angeles Times said that you did.

GR: Yeah, and I sent a complaint to them! We are in a theater! If I produce *Hamlet*, would you ask me if I lived in Denmark? Did you kill your father? No! Of course I'm playing with that and I know the piece is about that, but I don't feel... Real things that happen in a building that is called a theater, that is loaded with so many meanings. Things are not exactly what they are in the theater. Things are like they are but also another thing. If there's a sword on stage, it's a sword but also it's a piece of cardboard. So, there's many layers in theater, and I think in the worst of cases, *the theater of the real*—the theater that deals with reality— erased this quality of theater. I think we need to reclaim this, to claim that characteristic of theater being in two realities.

SC: Did you do one play for each of the 32 states?
RG: Not yet. We have done five.

SC: How was the play received by the audience?

GR: *Tijuana*? A complete success! [*laughing*] I'm kidding! I don't know... I have presented this play abroad a lot, in many different places, and in a particular kind of context—like art festivals and so on. It has been well received. Here it has been more problematic—and of course the play is for here. Many people criticize me for making kind of a *misery porn*—like I'm using the people to my own purpose.

SC: They always say that when we work with real people.

GR: Yeah, yeah, yeah! So, I don't know... For me, it's interesting— in fact, for me, it's good, There has been some discussion about documentary theater. If you present something in a way that you know people will believe, why you do it like that? How do we deal with that in a post-truth world situation? The president of the United States can say *whatever* that's not related to reality. Theater needs to work in that same sense—to make something that is perceived as real but it's not.

I wrote the text about the characters of Odysseus and Ajax, and how Odysseus is like a trickster. He's always trying to find ways to cheat people. The Trojan horse is the epitome of that. "Let's put a horse here. They will think that it's a horse but in fact there's not a horse." And Ajax is the opposite—he's the warrior who attacks frontally, without any kind of strategy. It's just his own power. Theater is very related to Odysseus, to the trickster, to the cheater. These kinds of values, I think, are values for the theater and theater needs also to claim that space as a place of tricksters. I'm not interested in literal theater.

Gabino Rodríguez (February 2019)

SC: You said that some critics said you were exploiting people but what did the audience think? Did the audiences in Mexico see themselves? Did they approve?

GR: It's difficult to talk about the audience because there are different audiences. There's a general audience in Mexico—it's a specific social class with a shared political spectrum, more left wing. In some ways people were celebrating me, saying, "What a commitment you have with your topic—to go there and live there!" And for me that was a failure of the piece! Is that really a commitment? Is it really a commitment to go six months there? If we go three months, it's still a commitment? Two weeks—it's a commitment? One day? One afternoon? When does something start to be a commitment?

SC: In New York I'm sure that my actor friends put on masks of Donald Trump and go out on the street and act like a clown. Could I put on a mask of President López-Obrador and do that?

GR: In terms of what?

SC: In terms of having the freedom to do it, of being allowed to do it, politically.

GR: Yes. Artistically, in Mexico, for some years, you can do almost whatever you want. That's not the case for journalism. If you are a journalist and you are making a work about some government or even about the economic powers, you are very in danger. There's a really hard-core situation for activists and journalists. But in art, you do almost anything you want because there's a long tradition.

SC: Can I support myself as an actor in Mexico?

GR: It's possible somehow to make a living as an actor. There are governmental supports—there are grants.

SC: That was going to be my next question. There's governmental support for the theater?

GR: Yeah, a lot, in comparison to South America. It's not Germany where you can work as an actor for one theater all the year, but if you are an actor and you are sort of lucky, you rehearse for a TV series in the morning, then in the afternoon you make theater, in the night you make a radio show. People manage to make a living more than in other countries in Latin America. And then we have the cancer that is spreading out in the world that is Netflix. Netflix arrived in Mexico. Actors are really making money for the first time, making real money.

SC: I asked Morris Gilbert if someone could produce political theater

Gabino Rodríguez (February 2019)

in Mexico. He said there's no audience. But I think you're saying you do have an audience—an educated, politically left audience.

GR: Well, the main university in Mexico has a department of theater that is quite important, and they have two venues—one very big that is full of audience. You can make thirty presentations in a row with—I don't know—four hundred seats full.

SC: *Four hundred seats is a lot! I imagine your work has toured the world. Is it received the same way in different countries?*

GR: It's changed a lot in the last fifteen years. A tour means a completely different thing than what used to be. There used to be a traditional sense in the festival theaters of getting to know different cultures through the theater. "Now we're gonna see an Iranian production." It was a completely different thing. Now, at the festivals that I'm interested in, people are not looking for what is happening in Mexico or in Cuba. It's really about following the artists who are doing this or that. It's more about how this particular artistic discourse is unfolding. The theater that we produce here in Mexico is very similar to the theater that is produced in Paris. Now we have global trends. Participatory theater is the same in New York, or documentary theater, or autobiographical theater, or how we rework with the classics. They're worldwide trends. Now the important question is how we look at particular artists, how artists challenge these big trends, these big zeitgeists.

SC: *When I was in school, many years ago, we were taught there's an American type of theater, a British type of theater, a Latin type of theater. You're telling me that that's not true now. Is that good?*

GR: I don't think it's a good or bad... I think it's impossible to... With the amount of information that is running from one place to another, it's impossible to keep national identity, local identity. It's not good or bad. It's just like—it's going to be like this. It's better to get used to it and to understand how to deal with it and how to position ourselves in order to dialogue with it.

Twenty or 30 years ago, your main interlocutor was your community, the local community that was coming to see your piece. And you were working to challenge that community, or to change a bit, or to get accepted by that community. Now it's different. You need to choose who your interlocutor is and how you're going to speak to that community. Now you say, "I want to speak with you and with you and with you."

SC: Yes... Okay, my final question. You mentioned Netflix. In light of the fact that there are film and television in the world, can theater ever be as important as it was for Shakespeare's audience? For Ibsen's audience?

GR: If the question is if theater could again be the hegemonic form of communication for many people, I think not. But I think theater is much more important than Netflix for many people. Many people—and we are spread around the world—many people still go to the theater. I am quite optimistic. We go to the theater in a very deep relationship with the art form itself. I think that it's not going to be popular again, with everybody queuing outside the experimental venues. It's a medium that has its own history and now it's like this and I think it's fine.

Jorge Vargas (February 2019)

"We fight with a monster. We fight from defeat. We are already defeated—but we resist."

Jorge Vargas is founder and artistic director of Teatro Línea de Sombra, Mexico, an arts organization that stresses social engagement, as well as artistic co-director of Transversal: International Encounter of Contemporary Scene. Vargas and his company have received many honors, including the Audience Award for Best Performance at the Exponto International Performing Arts Festival in Ljubljana and the Latin ACE Award for Best Foreign Production in New York. The Association of Theater Writers and Critics has twice honored him with its award for Best Research Theatre Director.

Steve Capra: *You've said that you've had many influences. You combine so many approaches to theater. We are so lucky today that we can do that! We can combine whatever sources we want in our theater. Our grandparents couldn't do that.*

Jorge Vargas: Yeah, of course! Because also art expands its limits and it becomes something very *porous*. It's more liquid, the frontiers of art. So we profit from that.

SC: *Your first group was Teatro Línea de Sombra. Could you tell me about it?*

JV: Well, with our first project, *Amarillo*, we made some decisions that later became very important for us. For example, we always talked

Jorge Vargas (February 2019)

straight to the audience. We were interested in that form of communication. We were there to *testify*. We become *witnesses* and we *testified* in front of the audience. We did not represent. We presented.

And it was the same with the objects we used. We used objects without mediation—not mediated by any process of artifice. We found an object and we brought it on stage as it was. In the laboratory, we tried to figure out how we could transform this object into an object with social meaning, political meaning. We talked about "an object that is intensively alive." It is the same object that we see in reality, but when we work with it, it becomes intensified.

We try to make a kind of theater without any intermediaries between reality and the stage. The least possible. Because of course, there's always something. We need conventions. The interesting is always to put on stage a kind of a tissue—in the sense of biology. You cut a piece of a tissue and you put it under a microscope. Not to say something absolute or to present truth about what we've found, but to ask about this reality.

Some people say that we are documentary theater—but we say "No." We are not interested in that idea of theater, you know? We are interested in putting a piece of reality on stage and opening its complexity. So we ask a lot of questions. Sometimes the questions that you ask are different from the questions I ask. We can only create a space to think about it.

SC: I see.

JV: We work with what we call *casos*—cases. For example *Banos Roma* is a case about the boxer—a former boxer—who chose to live in *Ciudad Juarez*, which was one of the most violent cities in the world at the time. We don't know why he chose to live there. We went there because when we find something that we are interested in; we always try to create what we call *question systems*. We ask questions about something and find one question that forces us to go to another place, to the context—to not stay in our comfortable theater. That's the way we start the process in most cases.

SC: You address social issues. I do in my work as well. Does our work have a social effect? Do we really have an effect?

JV: If our work affects—?

SC: Society.

JV: Society? I'm not sure. Discussing a problem is the only possibility of transformation. We create a space where people can ask questions

Jorge Vargas (February 2019)

about some things that are important to discuss. We didn't know what happens. I doubt a lot of the power of transformational art in general. I think it happens—but on a very small scale.

We fight with a monster. We fight from defeat. We are already defeated—but we resist. And so that's why we ask all the time what the meaning of *resistance* is today.

SC: Wonderful, yes.

JV: And because we work with reality, we have to ask about the ethical issues in working with reality, in working with people from that reality. For example, we knew about a group of women in Colombia, all of them displaced because of the violence. Together they built a small city. All of them lived in the *favela* of Cartagena de Indias in Colombia. They managed to get a piece of land that they bought with money from an international organization, and they bought a machine to make concrete blocks. They built their own houses—89 houses—and they called the place "The City of Women."

We were very interested in that event because we are interested in signs of life in the context of death—signs of life in the context of violence—and how we can identify and work with signs of life. So we went to Cartagena and we worked in the small workshops in the City of Women and we talked a lot with them. And at the end we asked them "We are interested in creating a piece about you. What would you like us to tell as your story?" They told us "We are very worried about the future of our sons. Because even if we can build our houses and we work a lot, the violence will still be there, all around. What is going to happen to our children?" So we crafted the piece around this fear of the future. The name of the play was *Pequeños territorios en construcción—Small Territories Under Construction*. It's about this fear of the future more than the story of these women.

So that's the way we work—with real facts, but also with a lot of subjectivity. We find that reality is not good and bad, but in the middle. The ethical problem today is not to choose between the good or the evil, but to choose the lesser evil.

SC: Yes, I understand. Jorge, I have one more question. Can theater ever become as important for our audience as it was for Shakespeare's audience?

JV: Yes, because I think we cannot really know the importance of Shakespeare in his moment. Marshall McLuhan said, a long time ago, that the theater has to be real or it doesn't exist. And I think the same.

It's not enough, fiction. It doesn't have any sense if it's not intentioned with reality.

I don't know what's going to happen in future. It's difficult to speculate, because the danger of war is more immediate and more urgent than ever. We don't know if there'll be a war in fifty years. In Shakespeare's time they had all the time in the world! No hurry! But today reality is *urgent*.

Marc Caellas (May 2019)

"I feel sometimes like we are some army, some poetic army. We have to keep doing it."

Marc Caellas is based in Barcelona. working widely throughout Europe and Latin America. His stage work often exhibits an intriguing relationship with the audience and is often woven into the urban landscape. He has created or co-created El paseo de Robert Walser (The Walk of Robert Walser), *which is a walking play,* El perico tumba la paloma (The Parakeet Knocks Down the Pigeon), *which is about the coca plant, and* Cuento ma vida (I Tell My Life), *in which the audience travels a route in a car. He's served on the faculty of Central University of Venezuela, the University of Barcelona and the University of the Andes.*

Steve Capra: *You've worked in many Latin American countries, as well as in Spain. Is your work received differently in different countries?*

Marc Caellas: Yes, because this idea of site-specific theater did not concern only the place where I work but also the people I work with. In each country I've joined a group of different performers, musicians, writers for each project. So, in order to avoid being just a guy that arrives there and shows his work, there's a dialogue between me and the local artists I work with—and the product is better because the play gets better with all these influences.

It's been different in every place. There are little differences. In Argentina, in Buenos Aires—it's a city where theater is a very important and social thing. They have an incredible number of venues—they claim to have more theaters per inhabitant than any other city. There is a lot of feedback between the artists, a lot of debate about each play.

And then in Colombia it's different because they are very strong in physical theater and music, and that enriches my work, that is more based in text or literal references. In Latin America, generally speaking, audiences are eager to get involved in a deeper way. European audiences are usually too distant.

SC: I can understand that the people you work in the theater are different, but are the audiences different, or do you have a small section of similar audience in every country who comes to see your work and can receive it?

MC: Yes... Maybe it's a little group of audience. I'm not doing commercial theater, so in a way, it's underground. Each city has this little minority of audience, who are eager to receive new things. As you know, you can access all the literature and the music and the cinema of the world without moving from your city, but with theater it's different. If you don't have the money to travel, the offer is very limited. Of course, you can watch something on your computer but you lose half the experience—or more! There are a lot of people under 40 in Latin American who are very enthusiastic to watch new kind of plays.

SC: And educated.
MS: Yeah.

SC: It's like in this country, yes.
MC: Middle class.

SC: But in this country it's a very small portion of the population that would enjoy a walking production.

MC: Yes, that's true. But I don't care if it's small! If it's small, well, we try to enjoy that. I feel sometimes like we are some army, some poetic army. We have to keep doing it. A walk refreshes and comforts and delights. It could be my desire to appeal to more people, in a hypothetical way. But, at the same time, I believe in the writer Hakim Bey, the anarchist. He talks about temporary autonomous zones—the group of people who are related with bonds, complicity, a group of people that you join to have this poetic experience together.

SC: What's theater like in Spain?

MC: In Spain, well—traditional theater is funded by government money, public funds. It's theater based on traditional dramaturgy, with characters and a plot—the idea that people in general have of theater. The problem is that the people who manage theater want to keep the theater *like that*. But, again, there are a lot of creators—we are looking at different ways of being on stage and it is difficult for us to get the venues, to have a place in the programing in the big cities. Of course, there are small places—independent, alternative. A lot of groups have more venues outside of Spain than in Spain, like in festivals. It's very strange.

This renewal that people in theater want—you don't see that in the institutions. We have old people—I mean old in mentality—who are managing theater and the money that goes to theater with old ways of thinking. They only support this traditional theater, entertainment theater, and think that the other stuff is *experimental*, not *a hundred percent theater*. It's a political fight, in a way, because in the end, resources are limited. How do you use this space for everybody if it's a public sector? You cannot really have some people privileged and others not.

SC: And how is your work funded?

MC: Well, my work is hardly funded—for instance, now, I won an open call. There is this festival in Terrassa, in Spain. It's called TNT—Terrassa Noves Tendències. They have an open call and you present a project and they select 15 or 20 projects that they fund and they open in their festival in September. It's a festival that's been going on for 10 years and it's very strong because they support this kind of different theater—you know, risky projects. That's one way. Then there are other ways—the private sector. There are also some grants in Spain for this kind of projects, so you can apply to them sometimes to get some funds.

SC: And so the money is given to you personally, not to a company.

MS: To me, yes, and sometimes to a theater that produces the play. I work with a theater in Barcelona that is called *Antic Theatre* that's very independent. It has a bar that helps to finance the theater. It's in a very public place in Barcelona, and they serve a lot of tourists, and part of the money that they make selling beers goes to funding the theater.

SC: The show that I'm most interested in is El paseo de Robert Walser—The Walk of Walter Walser. *You have a set of actors in different locations that the audience meets as they walk around the city.*

MC: Yes, in fact we just have an actress and a singer, and then the rest of the "cast" are people from the neighborhood, whom we call "non-actors"—but they are actors at the same time. The audience meets with Esteban in an corner or a park—we tell them "We're gonna begin *at that time, here*"—but they don't know where it is going to finish. They know that we will be walking one-hour-and-a-half around a neighborhood. As it goes on, there are interactions with people. Sometimes we give them some text—to a bookseller, for the scene in a bookshop, or for instance, with a singer who sings from a balcony—but others are people who we bump into their lives. Sometimes I talk with them previously, explaining that we may pass by so that they'll be prepared—and sometimes we don't say nothing and just see what happens. Sometimes there are really marvelous moments, like conversations between Robert Walser and the audience. And of course, the audience are never quite sure if someone is an actor or if not. It's a mixture of reality and fiction and this ambiguity keeps the audience very alert and very sensitive. It's like a game for them to guess: "No, that's true"—"That's not true." We create these little poetic moments in everyday life.

SC: And does the audience learn about Walser's life or do they learn about the community?

MC: Both, they learn about because it's inspired on a book by Walter Walser called *The Walk*. It's a very personal book that he writes in the first person. He writes about one day in a city from the morning to the evening. We choose some little pieces of text about him, some about the traffic, about the noise, about the beauty of the city. And they mix with the stories of the local people in each city.

SC: You've worked in so many different countries. When I was in school, I was taught that there is Spanish theater and that's one thing, and there's American theater and that's something else. Are there still different styles of theater in different countries—or has it all mixed together?

MC: No, I think there are different styles. For instance, the theater in Argentina has its own personality. There is this permanent idea of working as a team. Most of the scripts come from work between the dramaturges and the actors and the directors. Of course, afterwards there is one guy that writes the scenes but the process of creation is more collective. In Spain, in most cases, one guy comes with the text and then you begin rehearsal. That's one difference.

The other is that—for instance, in Mexico they are quite strong in documentary theater connected to political issues, a sort of theater that is not that common in Spain. In Colombia, music and dance are very important on stage—that's a main point. It's in the same language but because it's such a different country—Colombia from Argentina, from Spain—it has to be different theater because the social context is very different. You know, Europe from Latin America—but even within Latin America, north and south are very different.

SC: That's good to hear. I don't like to think of art becoming homogenized.

MC: No, no, no, no no—we hope not!

Marc Caellas (May 2019)

SC: In an interview in La Tempestad *[a Mexican magazine] last year, you used the term "intervention"—or at least, that's how they translated it. In this country that implies political theater, theater that is a political demonstration at the same time.*

MC: Well, in a way, some of my work is in that direction. That's difficult because one wants to create poetry and not a political pamphlet—we are not doing politics. It's difficult, you know, because political theater sometimes can be boring. It can be very, very obvious. I don't like to do that. When I try these political works, I try not to give a message but to ask my questions—to provoke, to open up, to show them in order to keep thinking, not with a solution, but with the aim of saying, "As an artist, I want to discuss this topic, but in a poetic or lateral way." That was the aim in that work about the cocaine and the drugs, because I think the legalization of the drugs is a capital issue in the world. It affects many aspects of our lives and war on drugs has been a big catastrophe for humanity. I tried to talk about that without moralizing and within the constraints of the common sense. I pushed things to certain limits, to the extent of doing something illegal, like giving some drugs to the audience.

SC: You gave cocaine to the audience?

MC: Well ... apparently, yes ... just a taste... As a theater director I feel like the guy that organizes a party at his place, so I try to offer food or drink to the audience—that I consider my guests—during or at the end of the show. So, in this particular case, at the end of *El perico tumba la paloma*,[11] Edinson [Quinones, an actor] goes to the audience and says, "A little taste?" The funny thing was that the guys that ran the theater in Barcelona thought it was fake. I never said it was fake or it was not! Only the people who tried could say if it was fake. They didn't ask me! The technician at the theater, the guy that was helping us with the lights and the sound, protected us without telling us. On the first day, the manager of the theater asked him "Tell me, but—they are not giving cocaine, right?" He said, "No, no, it's fake." Okay! I was surprised that nobody from the theater had asked me! On the last day, he said to us, "Okay, guys, I have to tell you, I protected you, so now invite me because I deserve it—I've earned the right to taste." And besides, it was good because it came straight from Colombia—more pure than what you usually get in Spain.

---

11. *The Parakeet Knocks Down the Pigeon*; the title has sexual overtones in colloquial Spanish.

Marc Caellas (May 2019)

But that was at the end of the play. The play had a spiritual part, too. It was connected to ancient rituals of the indigenous people that are the relatives of Edinson Quiñones, the actor. He's an artist from Popayán, in Colombia. His relatives are indigenous and in their tradition the coca plant has powers. It's connected with divinities and with rituals around gold objects in the Gold Museum—in Bogotá, there is this museum that's full of pre–Hispanic pieces. In this culture, they used that plant for many things—like, for food. The piece tried to confront how we see the plant in Europe—as cocaine, as a drug for entertainment—and how these people see it—as a plant connected to religion and meditation and rituals—and then the meeting of these two worlds and what happened there.

SC: I haven't seen Entrevistas breves con escritores repulsivos,[12] *but I thought about conducting this interview in silence and letting you do all the talking. That's what the interviewer in that play did—is that correct?*

MC: Yes, that was done in Buenos Aires, and afterwards in Bogota, too. It was based on David Foster Wallace's book, *Brief Interviews with Repulsive Men*. The journalist was a woman. She kept silent all the time—it was very powerful on stage. She didn't speak but she had *gesture*. It was played for only 30 people and people were very close to the actors. In a way it was a monologue, but it was based on the gestures of the *other*. Here again it was a mixture of the original text of David Foster Wallace with the biography of the writer. We were playing again with reality and fiction, so it seemed that a writer was confessing something horrible—that he is bad with women for instance—but in the end it was half-fiction. It generated an uncomfortable state for the audience that's always powerful. You have to take them out of their zone of comfort.

SC: And there were four or five different monologues.

MC: Yeah, and they were in different places of the house. One was in the library—one was in the hall—one was in the terrace. The audience kept following the journalist. It was in an old building in Buenos Aires that used to be the place where Jorge Luis Borges worked as a librarian in the 50s.

SC: In light of the fact that there are film and television in the world, can theater ever be as important as it was in 1900? Can it be as influential again as it was a hundred years ago?

MC: It's difficult because nowadays there are many more forms of

---

12. *Short Interviews with Repulsive Writers*, another of Caellas' productions.

entertainment available for people. But I think theater doesn't have to compete with TV or cinema. It has to go its own way and be radical and powerful and give the spectator a different experience. Because the live experience only happens in theater. You can watch TV at your place, but we still have the need to join with other people in a venue and where something unexpected and poetic happens. Maybe it's not so influential—when you read the papers, of course, the theater section is much smaller than the section on cinema or literature. But we don't have to care about that.

Of course, it always will be for a minority but maybe this minority may be influential. You look for that moment, as artist Francis Alys once said, that is social sublime, a collective emotion that may last five or 50 minutes, but those are the moments that I look for. The 40 people who are there for the play, those 40 people will tell that story to others about it afterwards. If the experience is deep and strong, they will talk to other people and they will generate a narrative about what happened inside them. That goes on and on—so it expends the effect. As long as we care for doing powerful plays, I think We'll reconquer the space. We'll get that theater again!

Ivo van Hove (February 2020)

"I think theater will be one of the most important art forms in the 21st century, because we live in the illusion that we can live in a community via our computer. I think that people will crave live experiences."

Ivo van Hove, artistic director of Toneelgroep Amsterdam, is known for a minimalist and expressionist approach to plays such as A View from the Bridge, Network *and* West Side Story. *He's particularly respected for his meticulous preparation. His many honors include a Tony, an Olivier Award, a Drama Desk Award, a Critics Circle Theatre Award (all for* A View from the Bridge) *and two Obie Awards as well as the Prijs van de Kritiek, the Prosceniumprijs and several other European awards. He was made a Knight of the Ordre des Arts et des Lettres (France) in 2004.*

Steve Capra: *In the foreword to* Ivo van Hove: From Shakespeare to David Bowie, *you wrote something very interesting. You wrote, "Whereas*

Ivo van Hove (February 2020)

politics needs to concern itself with the order of society, art attends to chaos. A failure to negotiate this dividing line has been obscuring the role of art and politics." How has art failed?

Ivo van Hove: Perhaps what I'm saying there is a very European thing, because art and politics are—*were* always closely connected somehow. We have this system of subsidies, which means that you have to apply to the government to make your art—and the government has to say "Yes." Sometimes in these days—more and more—politics demands things from art. You get the money, but you have to take care of this, this, this and this—which somehow I don't disagree with. But sometimes it crosses borders. The best art has always been made in total freedom, when people are not *obliged* to do something.

I'm a little bit ambiguous about it, because constraints don't mean that your freedom is more limited. Constraints, limitations, also give a new kind of freedom, because you have to discover how to make your point within those limitations.

But I'm still convinced that politics should take care of the order in our society—what we should do and what we shouldn't do. There should be rules, you know. If you break them—well, you break them. But in arts—I see arts as a subversive world. Why do we go to the theater? Well, I'm doing *West Side Story* now. Everybody who comes to the theater knows that there will be three people killed—something you wouldn't like to see on the street. Why do we come to watch a production that shows you three people killed? It's because these are the things that our nightmares our made of, and we have to—I don't know the English—it's good to *outlive* this. We have to sweat it out, you know? That's what the Greeks called *catharsis*.

What's a catharsis? A catharsis is when you witness something so intense that it cleanses you, you know? And what we'd rather not do in our societies—killing, betraying, killing your own children, even—all these darker things—that's where art reigns.

That's also the societal function of arts, you know? That's what we give back to society. We can give that back to the people that are living in the society and to the society as a whole.

SC: I neglected to congratulate you on West Side Story. *I saw the first preview. I wanted to talk to you about what happens in previews. Whose feedback do you take in previews? There are no critics. Certainly it's not just an extension of rehearsal.*

IV: Well, it is—it is an extension of rehearsal, but, at the same time another level is added. You feel "I cannot interrupt anymore."

Ivo van Hove (February 2020)

Normally I can interrupt and say, "Stop! Let's do this again!" I cannot do that because all these people are here. As a director, you are really put in the position of the spectator, of the audience. And you have to observe. There's much more time for reflection than during a rehearsal. In rehearsal I'm active. I'm doing things. And here I'm an audience.

I'm not going to read things on the social media because these days people react on social media immediately. I'm not on social media. But sometimes somebody comes to me and says, "Well, I loved it but *this...*" or "I hated it." It's all these things. I learned to keep my eyes, my ears and my mind open to whatever happens around me, but to make my own decisions. I'm quite autonomous in the end.

SC: There's a very interesting tension between the two. Once the show has opened, do you listen to what the critics say? Who influences you?

IV: No, the critics are not going to change my production. I've never—well, perhaps never say "never," but I never do that.

SC: Do you have dramaturgs that you consult with?

IV: Yes, but in this case [*West Side Story*] I did it without a dramaturg. But that's the first time, actually. I normally work with a dramaturg. And of course, there's my artistic team around me. I'm not making this production alone. I'm not a soloist as a director, you know. I rely a lot on Jan Versweyveld, who is my partner and also the scenographer and light designer—[*laughing*] who is always at the birth and the delivery of the baby! So he is really important. And also my whole artistic team, of course. I listen very carefully to what they say, but I have to make my own decisions at the end of the day.

SC: Your work is so interesting. There are critics who call you a minimalist and a reductionist. But the work of yours that I've seen has been effusive, with so many techniques.

IV: Yeah, there is one critic—Ben Brantley for *The New York Times*—I have to give him credit. He wrote a very good description for my work. He called me "the maximalist minimalist."

SC: I remember reading that, yes!

IV: And I think that's close to what I am. You cannot say I'm a minimalist because if you see a production like this [*West Side Story*], it's like not minimalism *at all*.

SC: Even more so, Network—*and* The Damned. *With all the many techniques that you used in* Network *and in* The Damned, *how do you insure that the production has unity?*

Ivo van Hove (February 2020)

IV: But that's my job. I make sometimes productions that are very pure, like *View from the Bridge*. It's only a few elements that I develop. This [*West Side Story*] is like a lot of different elements. It's more Wagnerian. And *View from the Bridge* is more Steve Reich. Both are great music—and I feel good in both worlds. I feel good creating these big symphonies, you could say, but also I feel good at working with a string quartet. But the work is different, because in a string quartet, every note that's not really perfect, You'll hear it, you know? In a big symphony, you know, when the trumpet is a little bit off, I will hear it, but audiences will not always hear it.

But that's what I like—well, not the most, because I like both of them, but it's what I also perhaps a little bit *invented*, that you can bring very different elements together as long as they are all there for a reason. I'm very much dramaturgically driven. I'm really driven by what it means—not what it *is*, but what it *means*—what the *function* is of a certain scene, what the *function* is of a certain metaphor, or symbol.

SC: *Well, your work has been called overwhelming. and you've said that you want a show that's as extreme as possible. Is being overwhelming itself a technique?*

IV: No, I never try to overwhelm. I try to get to the people's emotions and brains at the same time.

SC: *When I was in school I was taught that different countries have theaters with different characteristics—French theater is very text-based, Mexican theater is ceremonial. But* The Damned, *for example, was a French company with a Belgian director, presented all over the world. Is there such a thing as a national quality to theater now?*

IV: I'm proof that there is not, that you can break these barriers. When I got the invitation from the Comédie-Française, it was to do a production there, I thought "Well, why go there in this old-fashioned institution of people that are only interested in text declamation?" But then I came, and I made a deliberate choice for a movie script because how can—there's no text declamation to do. A movie script is always very straightforward. That's why I chose it. And then I chose *The Damned* which was, of course, very much a politically charged production. And, you know, they fell in love with it immediately.

They told me afterwards "Ivo, what you did now, that will have changed the Comédie-Française forever. Because we can never go back anymore. We will do the Molière's, but we know now there's more."

I travel all over. I work basically now in New York, in Paris, in

Ivo van Hove (February 2020)

London and in Amsterdam. That's where I create most, but we play—my productions play all over the world—

SC: Right!

IV:—South America, Asia, Australia, North America—you know—Europe, Russia—everywhere. I always had the ambition to make theater that would mean something for the universe, for everybody, for a Chinese person as much as for a European person. I'm not so interested in putting labels on people—like, he or she is Chinese, so that means *this* and *this*, you know?

SC: Well, that's just one example of your basing a production on previous material, which you do a lot. Why do you choose to do that?

IV: It's perhaps the downside of me that I never found an author that I could really grow with. I'm always jealous of directors that have found their author. It's something I should have done more. I've learned it now, though, by working in England and getting in touch with a lot of authors, like Simon Stephens, for instance, who I worked with now a few times. I learned there that they really care for theater. They sit in the rehearsal room. They listen to what you're doing, how the scene is developing. So that's more like a process. It's not like "Here is the play! This is it!"—and we see each other on opening night. I've learned now that playwrights also want to collaborate, which wasn't the case in the countries that I was living with, you know.

I think that's something missing in what I've done in the theater. I could have done better.

SC: But you renew all this material so well that it may as well be original material.

IV: That's the other thing! I started bringing movie scripts to the stage because before me nobody was really doing that. And I did it structurally for a long time and now a lot of people are doing it. So I opened the repertory, you could say, in that way. Movies became part of the repertory. You can bring them to the stage like other people did with novels, bringing *them* to the stage. I did that much later. I was not an innovator in that way.

SC: In West Side Story, *were you worried that the video would overpower the actors?*

IV: I'm never worried about things. Why should I worry? That is for me part of this whole world, how we create. I really am not afraid of failing. I don't like to fail. I do everything possible not to fail, but I'm not afraid of it. I'm not driven by fear.

SC: *Well, you've said that you've learned from what you call "bad productions"—and that's terrific, that you can work with that.*

IV: Yeah, because most of the time bad productions teach you the most. The good ones are good and then it's very hard—it's like when you try to reproduce a hit song and create another one, it will be nothing, you know? If it becomes a hit, it becomes something special, unexpected, that people have never heard—something beautiful, wonderful, extremely wonderful!

When you make something that's not appreciated very well, you yourself think, "No, this is not good enough, this is not good enough," you know? Then you learn to think, "Okay, How can I deal with it in a better way the next time?"

SC: *In light of the fact that there are film and television in the world, can theater ever be as important as it was for Shaw's audience, for Ibsen's audience?*

IV: I think theater will be one of the most important art forms in the 21st century, because we live in the illusion that we can live in a community via our computer. I think that people will crave live experiences. They will pay money perhaps not to go to the movies anymore, because as the screens at home become larger and larger and larger, you can have movies now on Netflix—and there will be other Netflix's in the future.

But the theater you have to experience *live*. And for that special experience, people will want to pay money—but not for pure entertainment. Because that you can have at home on television. You can have all the entertainment in the world you want. They want—they will have meaningful entertainment, which I try to make now with *West Side Story*. Meaningful but also entertaining. That's what they'll want to pay a lot of money for in the future.

Krystian Lupa (March 2020)

**"The actor cannot base his performance
only on the text he has to say.
The actor has to be spiritually engaged."**

Krystian Lupa emerged from the Polish theater and is known for developing a method of "laboratory rehearsals," taking theater to be a

Krystian Lupa (March 2020)

spiritual experience in extensive rehearsal periods. Some of his most lauded work has been adaptations of novels such as Bulgakov's The Master and Margarita. *He's been awarded many honors, including the Ordre des Arts et des Lettres of the French Ministry of Culture, the Europe Theatre Prize and the Austrian Cross of Merit, as well as Polish awards such as the Witkacy Prize—Critics Circle Award and the Gold Gloria Arts Medal.*

Steve Capra: *First of all, I enjoyed very much your discussion with Frank Hentschker last night.*[13] *I enjoyed your calling yourself a hippie. That's wonderful!*

Krystian Lupa: I was very engaged in that conversation.

SC: And I'm very glad you mentioned the Living Theatre. I worked with them for a few years.

KL: Ah! That's very good!

SC: You're well known for your method of rehearsal—your laboratory rehearsals. Could you describe the rehearsal process?

KL: We're extending the part of *wearing* and falling in love with the character. The first period is of course mandatory, when we are getting to know the text, everything around the text, getting to know the author. We wander in search of different paths. This is standard. I think that after this period you have you step away from the text or from the assigned scenes, and start your own journey with the character, treating it as a boat, a vehicle or a secret guide.

Actually, one of the break-throughs that happened in our character work—it might be more familiar to an American reader—was during a workshop of *Factory 2*, about Andy Warhol's group from the Silver Factory. It was in Krakow, in Teatr Stary. Back then, I used to work with that theater, but now it has become prey for power, so it doesn't really exist anymore.

We created our own script with the actors through a character journey. We spent the first month-and-a-half watching movies with Warhol and people from the group, who were the characters that the actors later took to the next stage of their journey. No roles were assigned beforehand. The actors had to find the character they related to the most and send me a letter with their choices. It was very intuitive work for me.

Then the next area that had to be filled was the *unknown moment*— the moment that didn't have any particular source in the text. It was

---

13. Lupa was interviewed at the Segal Center of the City University of New York.

the day after the premiere of the movie *Blowjob*, which caused panic and led to a crisis in the Warhol's group. We wanted to talk about this crisis, and because we lacked a source to fill in this area, we recreated that situation. The actors were so far into character development at that point—they knew all the relationships and conflicts—that we started to improvise different situations, just like Warhol did with his group. An unknown situation was recreated as if we were a duplicate of the group. We tried to relive the imagined situation. This event was a great experience and adventure for everyone. I developed an intuition to use this method of re-living a character's life in different instances, even in more familiar situations in literature, that actors have to fill.

The actor cannot base his performance only on the text he has to say. The actor has to be spiritually engaged. His spirit has to be advanced enough to penetrate the situation from within and rebuilt it from there. An event included in the text is not enough to start from. He has to build a whole world in his imagination, a world in which he creates that situation from the scratch, as if it wasn't written at all. We choose that way of work and take it to extremes. This leads to creating plays that are not only illustrations of literature; but that *rewrite* literature.

There is always a huge difference between the eventual text of the play and the original adopted text. We want to be faithful to the idea of the event and the *secret* of the event, but not particularly faithful to the dialogue that the author wrote. Of course, when you're working with material of great playwrights, known pieces of art that should not be altered, you have to act quite differently. But I am usually interested in taking on pieces that are not fully developed plays. Then I can give the actor a way full of freedom.

SC: Yes, you've answered my next question. I was going to ask you about the rules of adaptation. Last night you said you wanted to bring to the text what the author left out—and now I understand.

KL: Yeah, that was exactly the situation with Kafka's play that we were supposed to bring to New York.[14] We wanted to follow the clues in the story. When we encountered an abyss in the text, we discovered *veins*, or a *bone structure*, that led us to once unknown places. We started to play a role of a detective—that is, filling in the gaps of the event. I was talking about the dramatic process of creating this play and the play found itself in a Kafkaesque situation. The actors fell into a

---

14. Lupa is referring to an adaptation of *The Trial*, funding for which had recently been cancelled by the Polish government.

similar process as in Kafka's book. That allowed us to notice something about ourselves.

Subsequently, the theater was divided into two floors. The first floor was the floor of fiction described by Kafka, and the second floor was where we were in between the so-called *personal* character of the actor and the character of the *part* he's playing.

We recently workshopped an Italian writer's play, *Kaputt* by Curzio Malaparte. It's about World War II. We went even further and started to wonder what is actually the *secret* of the character. What is a character? Is it a character from a dream, that is constantly slipping through the actor's hands, that has to be constantly conquered? The spiritual adventure of playing the character eventually became the subject of our show.

I don't believe that an actor can be 100 percent in character for two, three, four hours of a performance. It's impossible—it is somewhat an actor's lie. For me, an ideal metaphor for that is *Slaves,* the sculptures by Michelangelo. They remained unfinished between the shape of a sculpted body and the stone. The actor doesn't create the character entirely. He becomes himself, he draws back, he walks the journey towards his character. The process of sculpting that body is never finished.

SC: Judith Malina would love to hear you say that. She'd agree with you.

KL: Thank you, thank you. Yes, they were very wonderful people, Malina and Beck. There are no people like that nowadays, especially in America. Their work was generational. It was connected to the sexual revolution. People had to *change their skin.* There was an eruption of art happening, and everyone was fascinated by it. Today it seems like the world died again and hid away. Artists used to reach further than nowadays. It's a pity that this process did not continue. That eruption felt like it would carry on, but societies got scared once more and got back to their comfortable habits.

SC: Judith's work was openly, expressly political. Do you consider your work political?

KL: I could say I had two periods in his life. I was a young man growing up in a communistic country. My first need was my own, individual freedom—and a need to see work of artists that dealt with the secrets of a human being. In my point of view, what I was doing was in a sense apolitical—but what would be political in this instance was the fight for spiritual freedom. The regime looked upon me as an apolitical artist, so I was not dangerous, and because of that I had some peace for a while.

Krystian Lupa (March 2020)

The situation changed in the '80s when I did a play based on Stanisław Ignacy Witkiewicz' text.[15] All of a sudden the foreign press saw it as an anti-regime play. Because of that, it was popular abroad—in France, in Germany. I wasn't interested in discussion or any polemics about political views. I was interested in the evolution of human beings through spiritual change. But from that moment censorship started coming at me, and from being an extremely apolitical artist, I became a political artist.

SC: I see.

KL: However, in this era that has started in Poland, the era of the breakdown of democracy, you cannot be apolitical even in the sense that I used to be back then. For a long time I was interested more in the spiritual, religious processes of societies and of the human being, as well as in his freedom—they are, in my opinion, topics of great political value. Currently, you cannot be just interested in these topics. When you are, you enter into a fight with the government to save our country, our society, from catastrophe. I became an artist who's strictly political.

SC: Krystian, my last question. In light of the fact that there are film and television in the world, can theater ever regain the importance it had for Shaw's audience or Ibsen's audience?

KL: We've always had the death of the theater announced in the past. We have moments in which different types of media take the lead. The audience changes its preferred way of receiving, they seek something else—these are all mysterious processes. We lived through a big invasion of the cinema and it seemed that cinema would be the biggest media, the media covering it all. It turns out that cinema is dying earlier than theater, and theater is coming back. It turns out the theaters are filling up, at least in Europe, with people who are thirsty for something more than just reliving the story.

Cinema is a type of media that tells a story, but even the most ambitious filmmaking is a recorded, immortalized, unchangeable story, not spoken by a living human. In my opinion, the secret of theater's immortality, its live ritual—because we always compare live theater to religious ritual—is *catharsis*.

Theater is a participation, it's coexisting with living human beings. Not a written down, pre-recorded or immortalized event. If an event is recorded, it's just an event, it cannot become a ritual. In an event that

---

15. Lupa produced Witkiewicz' play *The Pragmatists* in 1983.

happens live between a human who acts as a priest and a human who acts as a congregation, we are experiencing something that's not just story-telling. Story-telling in the theater is only an excuse. The immortality of the theater lies in the live ritual between the priest and the congregation.

Michael Blakemore (August 2020)

> "The best work usually comes out of the formation
> of a like-minded group of people who for a couple
> of years—maybe four or five, a dozen years
> at the most—act together because they've
> got a shared idea of what theater should be."

Michael Blakemore was associate artistic director of the National Theatre, London, for several years, after which time he joined the Royal Shakespeare Company. His best known work includes A Day in the Death of Joe Egg *and* Copenhagen, *both highly honored and critically lauded. His many honors include two Drama Desk Awards and in 2000 he won a Tony Award for both Best Director of a Play* (Copenhagen) *and Best Director of a Musical* (Kiss Me, Kate). *He was awarded the Officer of the Order of British Empire in 2003.*

Steve Capra: *You've been working in the theater for 60 or 70 years.*

Michael Blakemore: Well, I acted for a while, as you know. For the books, I acted for about 19 years, because, of course, it's very hard to get a job as a director, particularly as an Australian coming to England where the Oxbridge Mafia sort of gobbled up all the good jobs—with a degree of insufferable entitlement, it seemed to me. But I finally managed to get a job directing and it altered my career. In the course of two years, I got to do *A Day in the Death of Joe Egg,* Peter Nichols' play, which nobody else would touch. I did it in Glasgow, then it went to London and within a few months it was on Broadway.

SC: You trained as an actor, but not as a director. How did you manage to get those skills?

MB: Well, it wasn't so much I had skills—I just wanted to do it. I worked for a very nice, good director called David William and I was playing comedy parts for him in Shakespeare. He saw sort of a latent director in me—particularly in comedy, because, of course, you're always trying to invent business and liven up a given situation. He gave me my first chance to direct and it was a big success. And on the strength of this one play, I was invited to take over in Glasgow with another actor/director, Michael Meacham. Then at the end of my first year, there was a play about a spastic child, *Joe Egg*. It was a big success and I was off to the races.

SC: *It's really interesting that you say you didn't worry about the skills, you just wanted to do it, because there's really nowhere to study directing today.*

MB: I don't think you can study it. You know, like all these things in the arts, directing is a kind of native ability, really, the right disposition—and most of all, a curiousness about the craft and a wide perception that others are doing it badly.

SC: *Yes! Michael, in those sixty or seventy years, the theater's changed a lot. What do you think about all those changes in the theater? Are they for the good or for the worse?*

MB: Well, by and large, they are surely for the good. I mean, the subject matter of plays now permits anything to be dramatized and all pockets of society are finding their place on the stage.

The time I was working was a particularly good period for playwriting, with some very lively people writing new and very unprejudiced, untraditional, *unclassical* plays. It was a very exciting time—with Peter Nichols, John Osborne, Tom Stoppard… A whole host of very interesting playwrights came out of that period. I'm not sure now it's so good. The mechanical dramatizations, TV and film, are getting so good and they're getting so easy to access, they're taking away a lot of the territory which was once the province of the theater.

And you do lose touch as you get older, you do lose interest. I don't really like going to the theater much anymore.

SC: *The plays that you've directed are so varied—from* Noises Off *to Shakespeare to musicals and Noel Coward. Do you approach these different genres differently? Do you use different techniques?*

MB: No, no, not really A comedy demands truth, and the truer a comedy is, the funnier it is. You're not doing *Long Day's Journey into Night* when you do a comedy, but in many ways, the same rules apply. A comedy like *Blithe Spirit* that I did on Broadway, with Angela Lansbury—it's naturalistic in the same way that *Long Day's Journey into Night* is naturalistic, but they of course explore very different aspects of human nature. Truth is the important thing—in all forms of acting.

Michael Blakemore (August 2020)

SC: In Arguments with England *[by Blakemore], you make it clear that when you were working the British theater was in transition. Did the theater make a transition from an actor's theater to an ensemble? The reason I ask is that today many of us think of our theater as being a director's theater.*

MB: Yeah, I don't know that I like that much. I don't think I like it at all. I think there's the play, and there's the performance of the play, and the director is the man that mediates between the two and tries to get the spirit and the truth of the *word* translated into the language of acting.

SC: Yes, in Stage Blood *[by Blakemore], you say that of all the people in the room, the one least concerned about himself must be the director. That's terrific.*

MB: Well, that is absolutely true. You're a pair of eyes. Guthrie, who was a great director—hardly recognized now—used to say two things. He used to say he was the audience's representative and he was there to make sure the audience got the show they were meant to see. He tried to be, for the actors, an ideal audience of one. And that's what you should be.

When I go into the rehearsal room, I hope to have a pretty good idea of what I want to do and where the play's going. But I do my directing by looking at what's *given to me*, watching what's given to me and seeing where I think it's wrong and where it's going in the wrong direction and hopefully guiding it back onto the right tracks.

You've also got to think of a way of staging the play. You've got to think of some presentational aspects for the play. But, you know, the Belgian guy you mentioned [in an earlier conversation]—

SC: Ivo von Hove.

MB: Yeah—he's brilliant. Brilliant work. But he does put on to the stage everything but the kitchen sink. He draws attention to his work. And that's okay—it's great work. I'm not knocking it at all—it's brilliant. But there's a simpler version of theater than that, a purer version, which is to do with this great simplicity of four planks and a passion—people getting up in front of other people who could throw orange peels at them if they wanted to, and saying, "I'm not this person, but I'm pretending to be. Can I take you with me?" That's why theater has value, because the audience help create the evening. They don't help create an evening of film. Film is very important, but an audience at the theater contributes to the evening.

Michael Blakemore (August 2020)

SC: In both of your nonfiction books, particularly in Stage Blood, *you talk about the machinations at the National Theatre. You use the word "betray" a lot. How can we avoid those problems?*

MB: Well, the thing is, that the best work—which doesn't come often—but the best work usually comes out of the formation of a like-minded group of people who for a couple of years—maybe four or five, a dozen years at the most—act together because they've got a shared idea of what theater should be. And they become very influential. One thinks of the Group Theater in America and one thinks of the Old Vic, when Olivier and Ralph Richardson were running it. And then one thinks of the Royal Shakespeare when Peter Hall was younger and less corrupt.

SC: And if I can jump in, the Living Theatre and Judith Malina.

MB: Yeah, absolutely! And that's where the lively theater comes from. It's like a kind of tide. Like all tides, it comes in, it goes out. You can get very good individual work on Broadway, and on the West End—it doesn't always have to be in connection with a movement. But the great thing about a movement is that it provides shelter and continuity for a given group of people. They don't have to worry so much about their next job or their next project. They're part of a group that's on a quest.

SC: Could we talk about the critics for a moment? You criticize them in Stage Blood. *You wrote, "It's intolerable when a critic writes on the assumption that he has more intelligence and insight than the people he judges." Certainly an unfair review is unacceptable, but doesn't the theater need the critics to be a mirror for the artists and to educate the audience?*

MB: Critics are useful to the extent that they publicize the show. The show goes on, the critics see it, and the next day in about six newspapers there's a bit of publicity about the show. And there were some very good critics. Ken Tynan was a brilliant critic. He was so enthusiastic about the theater, and so truthful to his own emotional responses to it, that he was a galvanizing force. When I was a young actor, I used to run to read Ken Tynan's criticism every week because it was brilliantly written. And he wanted the same sort of theater that I wanted. There are some very, very good critics, but it's the pompous ones—

I have a go at Brustein in the book, you may have noticed. He is an intolerable critic—as if he's *needed*. You're not needed! We get on and do the work we do. We don't need his guidance. I don't like the idea that the critic is kind of the last stop on the journey and the most important one.

Michael Blakemore (August 2020)

SC: Concerning Kenneth Tynan, you said that when he learned how theater worked "he forfeited that innocence which enables the gifted critic to believe in the truth of his judgments."

MB: Well, the critic sees the show and he says, "Oh, God, this is well directed" because a couple of actors are being absolutely brilliant. He can make mistakes because a great many different talents put on a show. It's a very, very clever man who can arbitrate between who's responsible for what, but the critic needs to. He needs that innocence to write glowingly about some aspect of the show on the assumption that the praise is due in that area. But it may be due to somebody else. It may be due to an actor or it may be due to a director. Once you realize that, once you realize how *messy* theater is and that directors are very much dependent on their casts… If I have a show and I have one person in an important part who doesn't understand the material, then I'm in trouble.

SC: You've written that it's so difficult to discern the difference between the actor's work and the director's work. As a critic, I find that a serious problem. Can you help me with that?

MB: I think you're wise to acknowledge that. You know, I think criticism—there are people like Michael Billington, who's served 40 or 50 years on *The Guardian*. I haven't always agreed with his reviews, but he loves the theater and he writes about it with great respect and he writes about it conscientiously. The very fact that he has been read by thousands of people means he's made quite a contribution to the theater. That is not to analyze, in particular, his criticisms, because often I've disagreed with him.

Criticism is simply voicing an opinion, isn't it? And your opinion may be highly intelligent, might be very perceptive, but at the end of the day, it's an *opinion*. The fact that one critic calls himself a critic doesn't mean his opinion moves into a different category. Or am I being unfair?

SC: Well, certainly, my fellow critics sometimes disappoint me.

MB: I read more bad criticism than good. So when there is a good critic around, I'm always very, very grateful. Often, some of the best criticism I read is in a paper like *Variety*. They write to the point. They don't write to protect their own intellectual reputation. It's much more like *reportage*. Good criticism often resembles good writing about sport. The first job is to report the event and then, having reported the event, you can then determine the winners.

SC: In an interview with John Lahr, you said that Maggie Smith recognized that you had a comic instinct. Then you said, "It's almost like

Michael Blakemore (August 2020)

a conspiracy." That's great! Could you say something about this comic sense? I think you're saying it can't be learned. Is it just an instinct?

MB: Exactly! That's why I always trust an actor who has a feeling for comedy. And Maggie, of course, has a superb sense of comedy. Among one's friends, you know that some of them are funny and others aren't. That kind of day-to-day humor is not quite the same as the humor that a humorous actor can find in the material he works with, but it's obviously similar. With a funny actor, you can tell at once whether he knows where the humor is, where the contradiction is, where awkward facts collide in a *banana skin, fat man* way.

SC: When you directed the musical The Life *at the Southwark Playhouse, you had directed it on Broadway and you said to London Theatre magazine, "Instead of having two hundred dollars, we have tuppence." Do you have a word of encouragement for those of us who have a small budget—or no budget? How do we deal with it? Does the budget affect the artistic quality?*

MB: Well, it *can* affect things like the quality of the set because you haven't got enough money to do it. And doing a musical—you know, most musicals demand moving parts so you can get quickly from one scene to another. But I think you can do as good a work without money as with it. Often the trouble is that it can't travel. Doing a show on Broadway, it's sort of guaranteed a life because it can move. It can be recast and it can tour.

In some ways, the show I did at Southwark certainly rivaled the one on Broadway. It gained something from that incredible intimacy. When you work with low budgets, you usually work in small houses, and it's much easier to have good work appreciated by a small audience than a huge one. The minute you have to go to the back of the upper circle, other things have to be allowed for—projection, you know... You need very skilled actors like Maggie Smith to get to the back of the house.

SC: It's encouraging that you say that! My final question, Michael—in light of the fact that there are film and television in the world, can theater ever be as important as it was for Ibsen's audience, for Shaw's audience?

MB: Not at all. Not at all, I'm afraid. Why theater is important is that things can get on in theater which the various *sieves* of the commercial world would never allow through. The range of topics you can discuss in the theater... If you're in a poor theater—you could put plays on about anything. You can challenge convention. Whereas the minute, the more money is spent on it, the bigger, the more impressive the location or the theater, the more there are restrictions on you. That's the great plus of it—that it's not censored by money.

SC: *When I worked with Judith Malina, she would say, "I don't care if we have a budget—we're producing without a budget!"*
    MB: That's right! Exactly!

Robert Lepage (March 2022)

"All forms of art, all artistic disciplines, have to learn from each other and have to steal from each other. That's the logical evolution of art."

Robert LePage is praised for his work in several genres including theater and opera, as well as in multi-disciplinary forms assimilating puppetry. He founded Ex Machina, a performing arts company in Quebec at which he is the artistic director, in 1994. Previously, he had been artistic director of the Théâtre Français at the National Arts Centre in Ottawa. He's been named a Companion of the Order of Canada and he's been admitted to Canada's Walk of Fame. Lepage's international awards include the European Commission's Europe Theatre Prize and the Glenn Gould Prize.

Steve Capra: *In Canada you work in French and English, and I know that you work in other languages. Does the language of a production itself have an important effect on the message?*

Robert LePage: Yes, very often the energy is very different. Sometimes in our creations, we work with actors from all over the world, and some of them actually speak three languages. We worked with an actress once—she was a British actress, and she spoke perfect French because she had studied at Lecoq in France for a while, and she had worked as an *au pair* in Madrid so she spoke almost perfect Spanish. And she had three radically different characters, three radically different personalities, depending if she performed in French, in English or in Spanish.

    Language comes with, of course, a lot of cultural references that are very different, but also it comes with an energy. There's a way in the acting and in the delivery. There's a very, very remarkable difference, that's for sure.

Robert Lepage (March 2022)

SC: That's very interesting. Speaking of multiple characters, as I understand it, the first time you produced Needles and Opium, *you played all three characters.*

RL: Yeah.

SC: What statement were you making? What statement is a director making when you double cast that way?

RL: Well, when I did *Needles and Opium*, it was a solo piece—and a solo piece or a monologue is always about loneliness. If you're alone on stage to defend whatever it is that you're defending, and if you're the one playing all the characters and you're not relying on any other actors to help you convey what it is you're trying to say, there is like an overall feeling of solitude. Soliloquy always comes with the idea or the theme of solitude.

I created four or five solos. And it always—whatever you do, how many characters you play, whatever impersonation that you do during the show—there's always this kind of overall feeling of defending yourself or defending your cause on your own.

SC: Speaking of Needles and Opium, *I believe you restaged it after several years. Was that a drastic restaging?*

RL: Of course the world had evolved. It was 25 years later. We were in a different new world by then. There was a pre–911 version, there was a post–911 version. So of course, we went through very different times. In the personification of Jean Cocteau and Miles Davis—there was something that I felt was very unfair because it would have been black-facing if I would have performed the part of Miles Davis, speaking his words and trying to imitate his accent and all that. So I only illustrated it by shadow play. That was my way of doing Miles Davis. And Jean Cocteau was this very literate character who'd speak on and on and on and on.

In the new version, I thought it was a fairer thing if I had a black actor on stage with the other actor, who played Jean Cocteau and the third character. He actually would flesh it out. So it's great to have a body on stage to flesh out characters.

Every time I remount something, I try to change as much as I can. I try to reinvent things. I'm not interested in re-mounting exactly what I've done before, because often these things happen twenty-five, thirty years later, and you're a very different person.

SC: If we can go back for a moment again about producing in French or in English—what's it like to receive Shakespeare in translation? It must be, in a sense, easier. But you must lose something.

Robert Lepage (March 2022)

RL: Yeah, absolutely. That's the thing that's interesting about Shakespeare and why some people in the theater are addicted to original Elizabethan English Shakespeare. It's form and content. When you translate it, however well you translate it, you translate the content, and the form is as important as the content.

What you have to do when you translate, you have to find a way so that the content has the container, the form has something to say about the content. I remember working on a really interesting translation. There's a man here in Quebec, Michel Garneau, who translated *Macbeth* in a Quebecois dialect, very archaic French from when the French first established her colonies is here in Canada. He borrowed a lot of words that weren't words that we use in French today, and made it sound archaic, made it sound almost Scottish in a certain way.

I don't think that you could do a real faithful translation of Shakespeare in another language if you don't take that into consideration. You have to think as much of the form of the language as the content.

SC: So you deliberately distanced it.

RL: Absolutely. For example, the way people pronounce the word king in French is a *roi*, and *roi* in French has become a kind of a lacy word. But he changed it and used the old sound of the word—it's a really old archaic version of what a king is. It was actually very close to the spirit of Shakespeare. Actors actually had to learn these words. Even if it was the French language, they had to learn words, like English actors do when they do Shakespeare. It sounded very archaic, and it was a great experience. Of course, you can't apply this to every Shakespeare. *Macbeth* was a good vehicle for that.

In Italian, they say *traditore traduttore—translator traitor.* You have to accept that a good translation comes with treachery, with cheating. You have to have an agreement that this is not the actual translation of what it is but a better way of translating it by betraying it.

SC: Yes. Did Michel Garneau translate the verse into alexandrines?

RL: No, he didn't. Instead of lengthening and adding beats to it, like with the alexandrian, he actually shortened it, made it really tight and compact.

SC: In light of the fact that there are film and television in the world, can theater ever have the importance for society that it had for Ibsen's audience, for Shaw's audience?

RL: I think that in my generation, we were drowned in the television culture and the film culture. And it reflects itself architecturally. For example, in Quebec or most of Canada, theaters are made for film. You come in an old theater house and you have that cinematic frame, not that vertical theatrical frame. So in Canada we're still educating people theatrically. It's very difficult to explain that to people in Europe, for example, where they feel this natural evolution from antiquity and how theater evolved and how slowly it went into the cinematic language and the televisual language and the form it has today. It's the same thing with opera.

You've heard of, for example, the Cirque du Soleil. Well, circus came here very late and when they came, people here took it and reinvented it. There's something about that that's very healthy for a young society like ours. These means of expressions come to us and they feel very foreign—they feel very, very strange to us. And we take them and make it our own. That makes it a very, very exciting place to develop these new trends in theater or in dance or in opera.

SC: Yes. When I was in school, we studied Peter Brook minimalism. But you've moved beyond that using a lot of video. The New York Times reported that in 1991 you said that you don't want a theater that tries to become more and more like film and TV, and yet you use a lot of video. How do you avoid that?

RL: Yeah, all forms of art, all artistic disciplines, have to learn from each other and have to steal from each other. That's the logical evolution of art. It depends what you take from the cinematic language. Of course, I do use all the tools that people use today, and there is video and all of that—but that doesn't necessarily make it film. The thing I really borrow from cinema is more the cinematic, dramaturgical, narration structure. I am very much influenced by film writing to tell stories in the theater. I'm not that interested in doing close-ups of actors or trying to imitate cinema or trying to make it feel like cinema. I think that we can borrow whatever we want—depends what we choose to take.

There's a very interesting thing that goes back to the Greeks. When you look at interesting film writing, it actually borrows from the ancient Greeks and Aristotle. So it's not a contradiction to borrow from them and try to reconcile theater with that.

SC: You're so well known for using new techniques. Your work has always been cutting edge. How difficult has it been to get audiences to accept something they've never seen before?

RL: Well, I think that it's always a question of—how can I say—we try to create the theater that we'd like to watch, that we'd like to witness. We don't take into account "Oh, what would the audience want to see?" We trust that the audiences are intelligent enough to create with us and accept with us new conventions. But for that, you have to accept to walk out of the frame a bit. And that's the thing that's really exciting with theater compared to film or television, recorded or canned forms of narratives. It's a bit of a prison. You're stuck in a form. In theater, you could actually walk through the fourth wall if you want to. Theater becomes exciting and compelling when it cheats, when it walks out of the frame, when it does things live in front of an audience, that—freedoms that you don't necessarily have with theater or film.

This being said, there's a lot of possibilities in film. But it's a more magical experience when it happens in the theater, live in front of you in 3D. You come in with all sorts of conventions but if you trust the audience's intelligence, you could actually bypass a few rules and they'll follow you. Audiences today are very educated compared to like thirty, forty, fifty years ago. It used to be that people didn't know what flash forwards were and *mise en abyme* and all these things. They watch stories on TV now and watch jump cuts and they mentally follow all sorts of narratives. They come to the theater and they expect the theater to use that vocabulary.

Very often today's audience is at the end of the play before the actors are. I'm not talking about speed, I'm talking about the speed at which people understand the plot, the resolution, the goal. They're very quick now because they're very educated narratively. Of course, they don't know this. They would not be able to put words on this. What's really exciting is when you're at the end of the play before the audience is. That's what you have to focus on when you deal with today's audiences.

SC: Yes. Has it been more difficult to get the audience to accept new techniques in certain countries? You work all over the world and certainly the audiences come from different backgrounds.

RL: For sure. There are places where they are less accustomed to the integration of new tools, new technologies or different ways of writing. But it depends how these things are used also. Very often the way you integrate new mediums into performing arts—if they're too flashy, if they're there only for effect, if they're there just as a background, if they're decorative—that usually is an obstruction to getting the point you're trying to do. If it's part of the discourse, part of the narrative, if

Robert Lepage (March 2022)

it's not there just as a decoration but it's there to support what it is that you're saying—usually people don't have any problems with that. Actually they're very excited that you do that. It's people who use these new tools in a decorative way—even if it's in the background, you have the impression that it's in the foreground because there's all this busy stuff repeating what you do.

I remember that when I started working, for example, with Cirque de Soleil, we were working with interactive video where whatever actually happens, it reacts to what the performer is doing. It's an echo of what he does, a way of enhancing him in whatever movement he's doing. It's not something doing its own show on the side—it's actually something that's empowering for the performer.

SC: I see. Yes. You mentioned that your audiences are educated to theater, and I presume that as a social class, they're educated, as they are in America and the UK. Is that correct?

RL: Yeah, they're educated—but the education I'm referring to is not necessarily school years or that type of education. It's more about—they're very savvy now. They have people telling them stories nonstop, nonstop, whether it's on TV or film or books or on the web. A short thirty-second commercial is a narrative. They're so bombarded by that that they suddenly have an education. I didn't one have forty years ago, for sure—now I know much more about all that. That's why I say that societies have to be exposed a lot to that. And I think that most of the world is now.

SC: In fifty years, a hundred years, when critics look back on us, what will they say about our theater? Will they say it's as good as Ibsen's theater, Shakespeare's theater, Euripides'?

RL: Well, yes. I think they'll say it was as good. But we don't have an Ibsen or a Chekhov or a Brecht—we don't have a name to put on what we're doing right now, which I think is quite interesting. Maybe Peter Brook—but Peter is now from an older generation. But I think—yes.

The thing that helps us survive—and proves that theater is a necessity—is the pandemic. After two years, theater defines itself as a gathering place where people rub shoulders. And you have to be able to rub shoulders. It's not about communication—it's about communion, which is a very different thing.

In the same way, all the movements of the Beckett years and all that after the Second World War—the Second World War brought in a new kind of theater. The pandemic certainly gave us a two-year breather to think about what it is. What is it that we're about? What is it that we do? Why is it that we collaborate on the human experience?

And certainly the audience answers back with this obvious thirst for *gathering*. That's what people do after a crisis. You want to gather. You want to have a common, collective reaction to some other collectivity telling a story in front of you.

Kip Williams (March 2022)

"I see a great threat to television and to cinema looming in the future, but I don't to theater."

Kip Williams was appointed directing associate at the Sydney Theatre Company in 2012 and became that company's youngest artistic director four years later. His honors include a Helpmann Award for Suddenly Last Summer, *a Green Room Award for* Miss Julie *(which also won the Awards for Best Production and Best Digital Media Design and Integration) and two Sydney Theatre Awards, for* The Harp in the South *(which also won the Award for Best Production) and* The Picture of Dorian Gray *(which also won the Award for Best Mainstage Production).*

Steve Capra: *Before we talk about your work, I'd like to talk about the quality of national theaters. When I was in school, I was taught there is French theater, there is English theater, there's British theater. Is that still true? When I saw Ivo van Hove's production of* The Damned, *I saw a play based on an Italian movie about a German family produced by the Comédie Française in New York and directed by a Belgian director. Is there still national theater?*

Kip Williams: It's a good point. I think there's an extent to which it's true and there's an extent to which it's changing, and it's more true and less true, depending on the culture. I think for Australia, we're simultaneously the oldest continuing culture in the world with our First Nations people, whilst also being a relatively young colonial nation. And when it comes to the particular mainstage theater culture in Australia, there is a combination of the British tradition and a strong continental Europe influence, as well as the cultural sensitivities that are brought to bear, particularly for non–First Nations Theatre-makers. There's a kind of strong reckoning with colonialism inside the work as well.

Kip Williams (March 2022)

What's interesting about Australia is, you have that British tradition of the playwright being God and central, and the word being the kind of primary dictator of the making of theater, clashing up against the European influence of form being primary, of form being a kind of expression of content. It makes for a very kind of interesting mix. In the past two decades, you've seen a number of Australian theater directors of the likes of Barrie Kosky and Benedict Andrews have great success across Europe, the UK and North America for that very reason—because there is an interesting blend of those two traditions.

And as you point out, Ivo is similarly a director who pilfers from the best of various cultures to create a kind of new form, a new way of making theater. It'll become increasingly the case given the impact of the Internet on theater. You can watch relatively high-quality versions of productions. You can look at images of productions from all over the world in the way that twenty or thirty years ago, you just couldn't.

So I do think that each culture has its specific voice. Theater has traditionally been and will continue to be predominantly a geographically-specific art form. But I think the practitioners' influences will continue to grow and spread, and those influences will be felt within those geographic locals increasingly.

It is interesting that it's taken so long for mainstream audiences in cities like London to discover artists like Ivo van Hove. His *View from the Bridge* was such a tipping moment in London. You're seeing the shift in theater-making in that city from London-born artists like Robert Icke. Australia was starting to draw influence from Europe earlier than the UK was, which I find sort of hilarious and ironic given that [*laughing*] we're so far away from it. All the Brits need to do is jump on a plane for an hour and they would be able to see all this extraordinary work. And that started to happen only in the past six or seven years.

SC: *Yes. I've found the Brits to be determinately British in drama.*

KW: Yeah. I think that's very fair.

SC: *You're so well known for using video in your work, everything from* Miss Julie *and* The Picture of Dorian Gray *and the others. Can you help me with this? I am so old that I was raised on Peter Brook minimalism. And frankly, if you don't mind my saying, I find video hard to accept. All I want to do is watch the video. I want to watch the live streaming. Will I grow out of that, or has it been difficult for you to teach audiences how to watch that?*

KW: Well, Steve, I hope you feel differently when you get to see my work. I grew up in Sydney at a time when there was a number of artists

Kip Williams (March 2022)

using live video and they were very much responding to the anxiety of 9–11 and the war on terrorism. The video being deployed was very of the mode of *surveillance culture* and the kind of voyeurism that comes with that. One way to connect video to theater's spatial primacy—by which I mean that the one thing that defines theater from all other narrative art forms—is that it takes place in space.

My deployment of live video and screens is fundamentally about the way that they have a spatial impact upon both the characters who are juxtaposed with them and the audience who inhabits the theater. One example is the very first live video show that I did was a production of Tennessee Williams' *Suddenly Last Summer.* There was a huge white screen on a revolve that occupied the entirety of the proscenium, and the garden was on the other side of the screen separating the audience from it. The first half an hour of Mrs. Venable's story was a single Steadicam shot—documentary style, almost. It's a play entirely about truth, so deploying that documentary style gave this sense of *veritas* to Mrs. Venable.

This huge kind of domineering close-up that loomed over the audience at the front of the stage on this huge screen is a spatial expression in the piece. It sets her up as this god-like figure that you cannot question. I'm always thinking about the ways that the video is having an innate spatial conversation with the audience and the telling of the story.

I also am interested in the way in which videos can explode the theatrical landscape. It can take you into different architectural spaces within the theater but it can also take you into different imagined landscapes, psychological landscapes. Live video can do wonders to take you into the dreams and nightmares of various characters in a very theatrical way.

I think about it as a new form which I sometimes call *cine-theater.* It's like a mash-up of cinema and theater. It's extremely Brechtian the way that I deploy it. It's not like cinema. Cinema asks you to forget; cinema asks you to absorb the full technicolor reality of the world that it's showing you. The beauty of theater in the Brookian sense is that it exposes the mechanisms and in doing so, activates the audience to make that childhood leap into the imagined and thereby creates a story universe. Brecht kind of has that tension of both activating a story universe whilst deconstructing it at the same time. In all the ways that I use live video, you're always seeing the camera crew, you're always seeing costume changes, you're always seeing the mechanisms of

Kip Williams (March 2022)

the theater-making. So it is an extremely theatrical deployment of the cinematic.

SC: The Picture of Dorian Gray *is so different from* Lord of the Flies *or* Julius Caesar. *Do you approach these different genres differently, or do you approach them all through the screen of your style?*

KW: It's a very good question. *Dorian* is slightly different insofar that the relationship to the text had been bubbling away for some time. I had read the novel when I was a teenager and was very interested in finding a theatrical version of it. And the form itself, this notion of one performer playing multiple characters, was bubbling away within me, and they kind of collided—and that's very rare for me, for that to happen.

The standard process for me is to come to the text in an entirely open and blank way. And I read it and I read it and I read it, and maybe once in every 20 times I will have a lightning bolt vision for how it's going to be—but that only happens very rarely. Most of the time, I'll start to collect some kind of key formal dreaming on how it might work. Then, in working with the creative team and the cast, it is a relentless, rigorous interrogation and excavation of that text. I don't like to know anything about how anyone else has done that. I like to come to it in a very pure way. The main question that I'm asking in the first instance is "What story am I telling?"—by which I don't mean the plot, but "What is the expression of the work? What are the ideas and what questions does the piece ask about those ideas?"

Then the second thing I need to crack is the space that permits me and my collaborators to tell that story. I don't wish to be disrespectful or irreverent about words, because I love language and I'm very driven by language, but there's an extent to which you could be watching the production in a different language and you could still receive the story. I try not to think about it too much, but I'm sure people could look at my work and say, "Oh, those are thematic links."

SC: *So you don't have a fixed idea when you begin you work toward it with your cast?*

KW: No, certainly the initial stages of reading the script is a solo enterprise, and I come to the design team with some very clear ideas, which I then evolve. There are a number of set designers I work with very closely and those relationships are very important.

I used to come into rehearsals with everything mapped out, every tiny little gesture preconceived. And I realized over time that one of the things I was doing was blocking myself from receiving one of the great sources of inspiration that one can have in the theater, which is the actor.

Now what I do is I come to Day One of rehearsals with a skeleton for the production, and there will be a number of tent poles within that, that are very specific and a kind of arc of how the production will unfold. The set is designed as a playground for the performers, a space where they can offer inspiration, and I can garner inspiration from them.

Probably the biggest clicking point for me in that regard into that mode of working was doing Caryl Churchill's *Love and Information*.[16] It's the extraordinary piece of writing. There are seven sections with seven scenes in each section, and the seven sections have to be played within that order but the seven scenes can go in any order you like within that section. And there are ten scenes called the Depression Scenes, of which you have to use at least one, but you can use all ten, and they can go anywhere in the play. And then there are 16 random scenes that you can use as many or as few as you want, and they can go anywhere in the play. And then within the scenes themselves, it's just lines of dialogue on the page. So you, the theater makers, have to decide how many people are in the scene, what identity those people hold, what the location of the scene is. There's literally trillions of iterations of how this play can be constructed by the theater makers. And that form, in and of itself, expresses this story about the human experience of navigating information in an attempt to generate meaning in our lives. I'm very influenced by Churchill and the way that her plays are an expression of the content of the ideas that she's exploring.

Dorian is a different example where it's so technically complex that I had to—have had to preordain quite a lot of that production. But it still carries with it the openness in the rehearsal process for things to change, things to be discovered, and to find that collaboration with the actor.

SC: *It sounds as if* Love and Information *succeeded through something other than a through line. Was there something else?*

KW: Yes.

SC: *Yes. So a through line is not—What did Aristotle say? "Plot is the heart and soul of drama." Have we moved beyond that?*

---

16. He directed it for the Sydney Theatre Company in 2015.

Kip Williams (March 2022)

KW: You know, I have a complicated relationship with plot. I'm not very interested in it, I have to be perfectly honest with you. It goes back to what I was saying earlier about story. Plot is the mechanism to serve story. That's why I'm not that interested in a lot of television and film, because it's very plot-driven and light on ideas and revelation and philosophy. I mean, television at the moment is kind of incredible—lots of amazing television at the moment. But generally speaking, I'm not that interested in plot. If anything, it's something that I have to hold myself accountable for because it's important. The first play I did professionally for Sydney Theater Company was *Under Milkwood* and that is a work without a plot. That is a work that's about time and the cycles of time, the verticality of time as well as the horizontal expression of time. And so a lot of it was extremely challenging.

It's a piece that doesn't have a linear narrative in it. And so I had to find "What's the philosophical argument, or what is the philosophical line of questioning in the piece that will lead the audience to an end point of contemplation?" I found my own personal sense of that within Thomas' work, to do with the impact of time and the tragedy of time and the inevitable riptide of an existence and human desire to pull against that. So that was the story that I told. That was an incredibly formative experience, to be forced to focus so much on *story* and not *plot*.

SC: When future writers look back on our theater, what will they say? How important will they say it is? Can it ever be as important as it was for Shaw's audience, for Ibsen's audience?

KW: Absolutely. There are a number of quite mainstream contemporary examples of theater that have had profound impact on contemporary societies. The most mainstream example is Lin-Manuel Miranda's *Hamilton*. The social impact of the casting in that production has been felt in cultures all over the world. There's been a profound cultural shift on the back of that production.

And there are writers like Jeremy O. Harris and Branden Jacobs-Jenkins and, in Britain, Michaela Coel. Obviously, Michaela's work has had great impact on television with *I May Destroy You*, but she started in the theater. Her initial work, *Chewing Gum Dreams*, is a theater work.

So there is a piggy-backing off the back of theater that's happening through television and film at the moment. But these profoundly influential works are starting with theater artists and are informed by the innately political nature of theater.

There is something about the individual way that we consume film and television that somewhat depoliticizes it because we are not held accountable for our response socially in the way that you are in the theater. The very nature that you engage in a group contract to collectively make the thing in front of you real means that you are connected to all these people around you. You're literally physically sitting with them, receiving this work. You are collectively navigating and renegotiating the power structures before you within the story that is being told. It is an innately social political act to watch theater.

Will our work be as impactful and influential as Ibsen and Shaw? I think it is, in a different way—in the way that it's breeding that discourse, and then in some instances pushing it out into other art forms. But I believe that to be not a permanent state of transaction in the theater. In time, technology will advance in such a way that we will ultimately return to theater being the primary way in which we engage with narrative storytelling, largely because of virtual reality. If you, Steve, can be in Florida with such a detailed virtual reality head-set that it feels like you're sitting watching *The Picture of Dorian Gray* in Adelaide, you would do that. You would do that to literally feel like you are within a crowd of 1,000 people watching this thing. You will also do that because of the incredible visual storytelling possibilities that will emerge within that technology. The core of it will feel like you are in space with human beings who are telling you a story. That's what we want as humans more than anything else.

So I see a great threat to television and to cinema looming in the future, but I don't to theater. In terms of our particular age, I like to think we are as politically impactful and important as Ibsen and Shaw. We're carrying on the torch for future generations that will continue live storytelling and spatial storytelling being the primary way in which humans wish to receive narrative art form.

Mauricio Kartun (April 2022)

"Theater has become a resistance activity against the post-organic times, against virtualization, against digitalization."

Mauricio Kartun is one of Argentina's most prominent theater artists, applauded throughout Latin America. He works in many

Mauricio Kartun (April 2022)

genres—classics, premieres, children's theater, puppetry and many of his own plays—and he's associated with the progressive Argentinean theater movement referred to as "the new dramaturgy." Kartun has been honored with many awards, including four Ace Awards, four Theatre of the World Awards and the Javier Villafañe Award (for puppetry). In 2020 he was awarded El Gallo de La Habana.

Steve Capra: *Before I ask about your own work, I'd like to know about Argentine theater. I know that Buenos Aires is one of the world capitals of theater, but I confess I know nothing about theater in your city. Could you tell me about it? In New York, the Broadway theater and the experimental fringe theater seem to be in two different worlds, and the same applies to the West End and fringe theater in London. Is that true in Buenos Aires?*

Mauricio Kartun: Here in Buenos Aires, we have a huge theater movement—and that can be surprising to someone who comes to visit. But why should they be surprised? Some foreign friends are skeptical at the unending billboards advertising 500 or more shows.

The majority of classic theater productions are presented by the official theaters and they are offered at very affordable prices. Then we have the listings for commercial theater, where comedies and musicals are most popular. And lastly, we have alternative, independent, experimental theater, which is the greatest in terms of the number of productions. This type of theater is spread throughout hundreds of small theaters with subsidies from the National Theater Institute. Thanks to a national law, they have supported this activity for about twenty years.

These three fields cater to distinct public groups of course. Some audiences are very rigid, and they don't frequent the other circuits. It's very rare that these commercial audiences check out the *off* theater groups. However, every once in a while a successful show from one circuit gains prestige—because of an award or something—and receives a stream of new audiences.

In the last few years some of the larger theaters in the commercial circuit have added some successful independent productions to their program. These are often in lower demand. They offer only one or two performances a week, so as to not overplay them.

The most wonderful performances tend to have several consecutive seasons. To give you an example, my production *Terrenal, pequeño misterio ácrata—Terrestrial, a Small Anarchist Mystery*—has been featured for nine straight seasons and has had almost a thousand showings, and,

Mauricio Kartun (April 2022)

except for a pause during the pandemic, has not been out of the line-up except for a brief vacation break.

SC: In an interview for Teatro Nacional Cervantes you said that that you've worked in "independent theater" all your life, as opposed to the "official theater." Yet you have the stature that would be unlikely for a fringe director in New York or London. You have a stature that we might compare instead with the stature of Harold Prince or Sir Peter Hall, who are not thought of as independent theater. Could you say something about this?

MK: These are very different worlds. I don't work in other circuits because my staging method requires a lot of time and experimentation with space, and the artists need to be willing to invest a lot into it. No commercial theater hall here would produce a production like that.

The circuit I work in gives us a modest profit so that we are able to compensate for the months of work. We have excellent actors and I organize my groups with equal payment—my assistant charges the same amount that the actors and I charge. I also collaborate *ad honorem* as an executive producer, presenting shows in national and international tours.

SC: In the same interview you say that you rehearse for "six or eight months." Could you describe your rehearsal process? Do the actors contribute very much to the concept or is your vision fixed before you begin?

MK: I believe religiously in the virtues of making mistakes—in the sense of *wandering*, of making creative errors. The best things from each play don't come from the speculation or pre-scene design. They come from the practice that those creative bodies allow to flow during their performance. To make it flow there needs to be a state in which difficulty and the capacity to resolve it are made a dialectic pair. Recently we have gotten closer to the deepest and most surprising resolutions.

My job as a director is to nurture that flow and to contemplate the *templum*, in the oldest sense of the word, a space defined ceremoniously by fine rituals, a place that is regarded as sacred, even though ours might always be a profane and rude practice. We as directors, although we might not know it, are a vulgar variety of priests who establish liturgies and then read them aloud. But in order to read, one must wait until the scenic action creates its own discourse. Knowing that at some moment it will surge forth, I remain calm in that waiting.

SC: Also in that interview you use the phrase "the language of poverty of the theatre" and you say film has "a much richer language." Could you

Mauricio Kartun (April 2022)

say more about this? I ask this question partly because you've said that you dislike working in film.

MK: What cinema has offered to the spectator from the beginning is the gift and the privilege of allowing their eyes to fly, allowing them to challenge the unique point of view that theater proposes by showing a story from multiple points of view. That flight is one of the reasons that viewing cinema is so pleasing.

The language of editing, like any language, involves previous learning. The first cinema spectators didn't have that language internalized. It was alien to them to jump from one point of view to another. It was annoying, too, until their brains assimilated it and they were able to enjoy it. Today we sometimes learn that language before being able to speak, so that it is a form of communication that is as important as spoken language.

The language of theater is made from extremely simple-minded conventions, sluggishness and instability. It all stemmed from Franciscan poverty. Today it is exactly that poverty, that ability to do so much with so little, that is what produces such potent defiance—and a guarantee of longevity.

SC: In a presentation you gave on Hacer Teatro Hoy you say, "When we think of theatre we actually think of an alternative activity, a counter-cultural activity." Could you say something more about this? Not everyone in America or the UK thinks of theater as a counter-cultural activity.

MK: I think of counter-culture in the sociological sense—those values, trends and social forms that oppose the established norms in a society. In a society dependent on corporations, where everything finds support in the grand scheme, theater, which only requires a motivated body, a space and a light, becomes alternative energy. And it becomes more and more defiant. Theater has become a resistance activity against the post-organic times, against virtualization, against digitalization. It maintains its artisanal, rudimentary condition as an emblem of resistance.

SC: In the same presentation you say, "Theatre is a ritual of violence." Could you say a bit more about this idea? Is it related to Artaud's idea of the Theatre of Cruelty?

MK: No, I think of it as coming from a much more literal place. Theater is nothing more than an evolution produced out of conflict. All is found in its violence. Every work of art is always the flower of violence. Sometimes it is violence against something—society, confinement, or

Mauricio Kartun (April 2022)

the like—and we call it conflict. Sometimes this violence is against some person and it creates exterior conflict. And sometimes this violence is against itself with interior conflicts. In any of these three forms, and generally mixing the three, theater ritualizes violence, and puts it in the center of everything. It celebrates it. There are thousands of different themes in theater, but it always comes back to violence.

SC: Of the people you've worked with, the one most familiar to Americans is August Boal. Have you been very influenced by Boal? How are you preserving, or extending, or adapting the principles of the Theatre of the Oppressed?

MK: Yes, he was my teacher in the 1970s. I worked as an actor in his group, and we were friends. I am still very good friends with Cecilia, his widowed wife. I don't practice any of his techniques, but I preserve some of the basics of his plays—they amazed and inspired me when I saw the first few shows. Augusto was a landmark of my generation and a very provocative mind.

SC: You're known for your political thought. You're associated with socialism and, in Sacco and Vanzetti at least, anarchism. What's more, you've worked through a dynamic period of Argentine politics. Have you ever had to confront government censorship?

MK: When the military dictatorship rose to power in 1976, I worked with Boal and with another beloved artist, the filmmaker Pino Solanas. Both were aware of the risk that staying posed to them and went into exile. Both very generously offered me the chance to travel with them and help them in Europe. It might have been my denying nature, or my naivety, or for the fear of leaving it all behind, but I decided to stay here instead.

Those were dark and silent years. All of my activity in that militant theater that I had been practicing in was stifled. Just as our saying goes, we must hold out and weather the storm.

In the meanwhile, I premiered *Chau Misterix*,[17] a piece written in the workshop of one of my other teachers, Ricardo Monti. It might've been the most important workshop of my theater experience. In that production, far from all *opinion* theater, I got into a theme very present in my mind: my neighborhood from my childhood. With the return of democracy in 1983, I joined political theater with this other obsession and in that mix appeared something which critics consider to be my style.

---

17. Bye, Misterix (an Argentine comic book character).

Mauricio Kartun (April 2022)

SC: What are the principles behind your staging? Has the development of your stage technique corresponded to the development of your political thought? Can we draw parallels between the two?

MK: My generation's theater has been like Bertolt Brecht's theater. I incorporated a lot of that. In some way I practice distancing, although for reasons that are somewhat vulgar: love for the variety show, for the circus, and for poetics without a fourth wall. Aesthetics is a place of identity. Sometimes artists disguise themselves. They assume different looks, and they don't understand that in this simulation they sacrifice its marvelous source.

Writing can be analogous to thought. We writers don't write what we think—we think as we write. Much of what we know is revealed to us in the strange act of reasoning through a string of words, of tying ideas together and reflecting on them. Images, words, and ideas become one.

SC: You give some of your plays, like Sacco and Vanzetti, *to other directors. Is it difficult to give to someone else the control that a director has?*

MK: I was an *author de escritorio*—a *desk author*—for twenty years. When we premiered *Sacco and Vanzetti* I still hadn't directed yet. I finished the text and patiently began the work of finding a director for it. It was strange, because I had studied more in the field of directing than in drama. I started to transition to directing. When I did this, I added a mixed system to my repertoire. I now premier my new pieces myself and I try to maintain them as long as possible. But once attendance starts dwindling and it is no longer reasonable to do that, I leave them in the hands of those who would experiment with them—as long as the project offers some artistic prospects, of course.

SC: In your Hacer Teatro Hoy presentation you say, "Theatre has an extraordinary future" but that "achieving this survival is increasingly difficult" because of the cinema. In light of the fact that there are film and television and internet in the world, can theater ever regain the importance it had for Shakespeare's audience, or for the Spanish Golden Age audience?

MK: Never the same importance. Theater had a monopoly on telling stories for centuries. It has a different type of importance now, but nonetheless far-reaching. Theater is the great language, the mythical, the invariable and therefore the eternal one. It is a combination of two of the biggest intelligences: on one side, the narrative intelligence, and on the other, the mimetic intelligence of the actor, which finds the greatest expressiveness. Here there are no tricks or cuts and one's memory must be spectacular.

In cinema's near future, the majority of their performances will be animations, because it's easier and profitable for the industry—and that is the only thing that matters to them. Just as movie theaters are starting to disappear, the bodies on the screen will slowly disappear too, replaced by avatars. Why do we need actors in the first place if in a virtual setting all that really matters is plausibility? It's easier to achieve that with an actor who is connected to sensors.

Cinema will still surprise us with its effects. And the eternal theater will continue to surprise us with its magical ability to do so much with almost nothing. The challenge now is about continuing to awe the audience and this challenge will grow with time. Theater will live on but it will need acting that will shock us, something that will deliver that final touch. The spectacle won't be in simply receiving a story. Rather, it will be found in the wonder that those bodies can capture in order to express it. We'll go to the theater to reconnect to the poetic power of the human body.

Christiane Jatahy (April 2022)

> "Theater for me does not make sense if it's not about nowadays. I have to access it by what's happened around me. The classical text is the way that I go into what's happening in the world now."

Christiane Jatahy works extensively in Brazil and Europe and is widely praised for her interdisciplinary productions such as Julia *(based on Strindberg's* Miss Julie). *She is an associated artist at Centquatre-Paris, at the Odéon—Théâtre de l'Europe, at the Piccolo Teatro de Milano and at Schauspielhaus Zürich. She's a member of the Comédie-Française and in 2022, she was awarded the Golden Lion Award at the Venice Biennale Teatro. Jatahy is the founder of the theater company Companhia Vértice de Teatro, Brazil.*

Steve Capra: *Christiane, before we talk about your work, could you tell me about Brazilian theater just a bit?*

Christiane Jatahy: Now we are in a very difficult moment here. It's very, very complex because of this government. In the theater, it's hard to do some things because of covid, but also because of the fight from

Christiane Jatahy (April 2022)

this government with the artists. It's really complicated to do something, to find the structure for your work.

My case is different because I'm working in Europe—although now I'm here in Brazil. But most of my friends here are doing *streaming*. The theater is in a really complicated moment—but everything in Brazil is now. It's very hard, what's happened. The president—he's a crazy man.

SC: In New York and London, there's a split between conventional, realistic theater and the avant-garde. They seem to be in two different worlds. Is that true in Brazil?

CJ: Yes, but not completely. For sure, there is a theater that is more conventional, more traditional. But the boundary—it's not one or the other. It's possible to find in the boundary some work that is in a very good relationship with the audience in a way that you really cannot have with popular theater, work that has communication between the two territories. I know that in the United States they are separated, but here, no, it's not so much.

SC: That's good to hear. Christiane, you've said that your work concerns the frontiers between film and theater and between reality and fiction. That's what I'd like to talk about. You combine film and theater in a variety of different ways and in very complex ways.

CJ: Yes, I work at the border between theater and cinema, and also at the border between reality and fiction and at the border between the characters and the actors. I also try to work in terms of the relationship with the audience.

I studied theater, journalism, philosophy—and also cinema. So I think that these two territories—cinema and theater—are inside of me. I ask myself how I can use in the theater some procedures—some dispositives—that we use in the cinema. So it's not only that I use projections, but the language of the cinema can be part of theater. I try to create a dramaturgy of which the cinema is really part. The cameras, the montage of the cinema, the presence of the cameras are part of the fiction. The projections can help not only to see the other's point of the view but really to complete the script of the play.

I work on a lot of levels when I'm working with these boundaries to create new possibilities, to go deeper into the subject that I'm talking about in the play.

SC: These must be new techniques for most of your audiences. Is it difficult to get them to accept these very experimental techniques?

Christiane Jatahy (April 2022)

CJ: No. The relationship with the audience is interesting. I really think a lot about how I can put the audience inside of the play, but not in the conventional sense of "participatory theater." I really think about the point of view of the audience. The web that I create between the cinema and theater provokes the audience to feel part of the play, to complete what I'm saying in the play. Some of the technology that I use to do this is innovative because I'm not only using cinema on stage—a lot of people use cinema—but I'm creating a new relationship with the cinema.

The relationship with the audience is very stimulating. For example, in New York you saw *What If They Went to Moscow?* The play [based on Chekhov's *Three Sisters*] is cinema and theater at the same moment. It's a challenge because it's four hour long. You have seen the film and the play. One part of the audience sees the play and the other part sees the film—and then switch. It's not just projection on the stage—it's cinema. The cinema is a kind of *utopia* of the theater and the theater is a *utopia* of the film. When you see the film, you imagine the play and when you see the play, you imagine the film.

I give audience space so that they feel like the three sisters. When you are in one place you imagine what you desire when you talk about the other place. I split the audience just to create this feeling—the feeling of staying in a place, or in a play, or in a film, and imagining what's happening in the other space. The theater does not exist in this case without the film and the film does not exist without the theater.

The camera is on the stage and it's really part of the fiction, the characters. For example, Vershinin is the man who brings the camera. Masha falls in love with the cameraman. So when she looks at the camera, she looks at the audience in the cinema. There are a lot of levels in this relationship between the cinema and theater. And in each play, change the form, I change the way that I work. I don't use the same *dispositive* in all plays. I change the procedures in each play depending on the content.

SC: *You use the word "dispositive." Are you talking about stage techniques or administrative techniques? I haven't heard the word used in regard to the theater.*

CJ: It means a social structure. The dispositive is a kind of bridge between the actors and the audience. It's social and political. It's also *dispositive* in the sense that I can provoke myself. It's about how I can go deeper into the content that I'm working on in the play.

Christiane Jatahy (April 2022)

SC: You set What If They Went to Moscow? *in Brazil. When you change the setting of a play, what are the challenges there? You must lose something—in this case I imagine you would lose a 19th century formality. But you must gain something too. It must be a balancing act. Could you say something about adapting a script into a new time, a new country?*

CJ: Theater for me does not make sense if it's not about nowadays. I have to access it by what's happened around of me. The classical text is the way that I go into what's happening in the world now. When I use a classical text, I use in a lot of ways. First, I understand that the audience have this memory inside of them. So I use the memory, I use collective memory. It's like historical memory. I don't say that my version is the only version. You have a point of view about this memory and the other has a different perception. I use this as a boat to go into the content. For sure is an adaptation. But this adaptation uses the past to think about the present and to change the future.

For example, to speak again of *Three Sisters,* or to speak of Strindberg's *Miss Julie*—at the end of the two plays, the actresses ask to audience—or ask themselves—what they can do to change, not to repeat the same problems.

In *Julia,*[18] for example, at the end of the play, there are also a lot of levels. The first level is Strindberg's story, but the story *now*. The second level concerns the actors who are making the film about this story. The third level is how this story affects the actors, how they become closer and closer to the reality. The tension lines between reality and fiction also affect the actors and the relationship between them. You never know if the actors are acting or not. For sure they are acting, but I play with this.

The third level of *Julia* is how they are affected by the fiction and their feelings about this are revealed in the end of the play to finish the story. Julia, the actress and also the character, say to audience that they don't want to create this ending again. And they ask the audience what they can do now. We—she and us—do not have an answer for changing the ending. For sure we're not waiting for an answer from the audience but only for us all to think about this.

So it's not an adaptation on just one level. It's on a lot of levels connecting the classical text with reality *now*.

SC: Christiane, I know that you use documentary and interview a lot in The Lingering Now, *your adaptation of* The Odyssey. *How do you use interviews and documentary in the production?*

---

18. Jahaty's production, based on Strindberg's *Miss Julie*.

Christiane Jatahy (April 2022)

CJ: It depends on the work. As I said, I change a lot. As a journalist I'm very interested in what's happened in reality to film the fiction. And I also use the interviews and the documentaries to prepare the audience for some works. For example—again about *Three Sisters*—I did a documentary before to starting the work, a documentary called *Utopia. com*. For this documentary I asked a lot of immigrants, refugees, people who changed their country, about the idea of *home*, the idea of *utopia* and what they want to change in their lives. This was to prepare to do the adaptation of *Three Sisters*, but finally it became a documentary, a film. It's part of the development of *What If They Went to Moscow* that is mixed documentary and fiction.

I use the cinema in another way in *The Lingering Now*. When you enter the theater there is a very big screen in the room. I project the film, a film that we made in a lot of countries—in Palestine, in South Africa, in Greece, in Amazonia, Brazil, and in Lebanon. What I do in this film is to ask the real Odysseyers, Ulysses' men and women who live their odyssey now, what happened in their lives to create their Odyssey.

In French the name is *le présent qui déborde*—that means the present that overflows, that never stops. In this *Odyssey* I use the text from Homer to bring in fiction so that they are themselves but they are also the characters of the *Odyssey*. They use this fiction for to tell us about their lives. In each country *Odyssey* is in a new phase, in a new moment of the *Odyssey*.

It's between theater and cinema. It's a documentary but also it's fiction because they are acting the Homer text. The moment when they leave the fiction and enter reality is very subtle. The way that I show this is to explain the film and the performers. The actors and the actresses are in the middle of the audience, but the audience doesn't notice. But when they react to the film it changes the film. The characters in the cinema start to dialogue with the actors in the middle of the audience. The theater brings the film to present and future. The live actors give a hint of how maybe the present of the theater can change the past of the film. So this relationship that we've created with the film and the odyssey of this person has become our odyssey. That is the way that I always work—how the present can change everything. Maybe it can change a bit the past that it seems impossible to change.

SC: *Now I understand why you sometimes use the word installation to refer to your work. It's much more than a stage play. It's a whole experience.*

CJ: Really.

Stan Lai (April 2022)

SC: Cristiane, my last question. In light of the fact that there is film in the world, and television and the Internet, can theater ever have the importance that it had for Shakespeare's audience or for Gil Vicente's audience? Can it ever have that importance again in terms of affecting society?

CJ: I had a hope, when the pandemic started, that because of this solitary experience, each one in his or her home, the collective moment which only exists in theater would prove again to be very important. The collective moment that happens only in the theater can be very important. It's important to be in a collective moment to see something. And my experience after the pandemic—I showed some plays in Europe, but not in Brazil yet—was that it was very touching to see how the audience reacted to being together again seeing a play.

For me it's always very political. It's always a political thing that you are saying. It's impossible when you are in this place, in this kind of *agora*, not to think *together* about some ideas. This is very revolutionary, this is political. As human beings we need this moment to feel that there's someone who is on your side and sees the same and thinks the same. You can find this in the Greek theater, you can find this in the Shakespeare period, as you said. It's not only to see something, it's to be part of something, it's knowing that this is part of me.

It's again about the utopia. You only can change the world if you do it collectively, *together*. This microcosm called theater, the microcosm of the society, is the space to do this. So even you have a feeling that we've lost something because of streaming and television—not the cinema because the cinema is different—I don't believe that. I think that we will continue to need this space because it's the place where you can find the *other* and the place where you can think *together* about these things.

Stan Lai (April 2022)

"The way I work with improvisation, it's all very specific. There's no general way to work with improvisation."

Stan Lai is one of the most honored directors in the Chinese-language theater, and works as well in the United States. He is founder and artistic director of the Performance Workshop in Taipei and co-founder of the Wuzhen Theatre Festival. In 2015 he founded Theatre Above in Shanghai, devoted to producing his plays. His many honors include two

Stan Lai (April 2022)

National Arts Awards and the Grand Cordon, Order of Brilliant Star (both Taiwan). He's been named The Most Influential Man of the Year in the Field of Culture by Newsweek China and he's been admitted to the Chinese Theater Hall of Fame.

Steve Capra: *I'm interested in your rehearsal period. I'm interested in knowing how you work as a director when your actors are improvising in rehearsal.*

Stan Lai: It's an interesting phenomenon. The work materializes slowly through the rehearsal process. The way I work with improvisation, it's all very specific. There's no general way to work with improvisation. You start with an idea that can be extremely abstract and vague, or it can be extremely concrete. You can already even sort of know what's going to happen. But when you give it to your actors, you spend time exploring who they are.

Once the parameters are set, they improvise. We start from vague ideas and then get into more concrete things. Blocking or whatever scenic needs there are materializes during the process. "We need a chair here. We need an hourglass there." Specific things start coming. And then as they come, they stimulate me to think of other things that are more designed. "Okay, well, let's make a five-foot hourglass and put it right there." And then I'll tell the actress "There's a five-foot hourglass there—go!" And so they'll adapt. The direction we go to is set by me, and is purposely vague so that we can all explore together.

There is a sort of a work ethic where improvisation implies democracy or decentralization of the process. But for me, it's never been that way. That's how my process evolved until to this day. The actors are free to do whatever they want during improvisation, but I control it very carefully, and I give them parameters that are very small. Within the small parameters, they are able to function at a high level. Given huge parameters, they don't know what to do.

SC: Absolutely. I can understand that completely for my own work as an actor.

SL: Thank you so much. If I say, "Steve, we're talking about plants. Go!" you don't have an idea whether that's connecting with what I'm thinking of or not. It's just a shot in the dark.

Later on in my career, I gave out very detailed outlines to the actors. For my play *The Village*, 48 scenes were already laid out. The actors whom I worked with for many years trust me, so they just come to the rehearsal and they don't even know what character they're going to play.

And *I* don't know what character they're going to play. And through the first week or so, they find their place. We do different improvs on different scenes with different combinations of actors, and they see and I see—it's like an extended casting period. Then they all get to where they should be and maybe other characters appear from that.

Secret Love in Peach Blossom Land is probably my most well-known play. It's about two theater groups who are fighting for the stage for a rehearsal. One is a serious play, one is a comedy, and I originally had six actors assigned to it—three main and three sort of utility who weren't professionals. Those were the days when we worked with whoever we could. Every time I wanted to rehearse those scenes, these three guys didn't show because they're not professionals. We were very tolerant of that. And then we realized we didn't need them—this whole play would be done with just three actors.

The whole Peach Blossom Land part is just for three actors—there can't be any more. So the fact that they didn't show was a blessing for us. But our work ethic is that you don't fire these people. They really want to contribute. So we created these other characters. There's this character called The Lost Woman, and she's become one of the most controversial characters I ever wrote. Everyone talks about her. People have written even theses about whether she should be in the play. She's one of those actors who didn't show for those rehearsals.

SC: *Stan, I've seen your film of* Secret Love in Peach Blossom Land *and it was terrific. Even though I didn't understand the Chinese, it was engaging, and I laughed through a lot of it.*

SL: In the early days the improvisations would be more free. I've done a few plays where it's more of a vignette style. The first play I worked with a semi-professional group is called *Plucking Stars*. It's about families of the mentally retarded. We were approached by a teacher in Taipei who saw my first play and said, "Can you do a play for us?" And I said, "Sure." We had a group of 16 semi-professionals and amateurs. We would spend as much time as we could in the school that the man ran, observing things, and then come back to the studio at night and act out what we saw. And then I would be devising scenes.

It ended up being 16 separate scenes with connecting characters. There's a structure, but it's vignettes. People said, "Oh, this improvisatory technique works well for this sort of vignette style, but can it make a unified, structured play?" And I thought, "Sure, it can." And so I started doing that, too. If you've worked through improvisation, you can't say, "Okay, now let's reblock this thing." It will not listen to you. If you try to mess with the organic process of improvisation by adding blocking or adding characters, it doesn't work.

SC: In Secret Love in Peach Blossom Land *you created that complex structure first and then gave it to them.*

SL: They knew that for sure. That's the power of improvisation. That's what you can't beat as a writer working on your own. If you have actors like these who are so sensitive and understanding—

SC: And so gathered as a cast—

SL:—and so gathered as a cast and unified with what I'm thinking, it's like our minds are one. At least our direction is one. Our minds can never be one, but at least we're going in the same direction.

SC: You gave the most interesting interview to Critical Stages[19] *about four years ago, and you talked about creating theater in Taiwan. You said that in Taiwan, unlike China, there was no style to react against. It was like working in a vacuum. And I read that and I thought, "That's great! Finally, here's a theater without expectations, that refers to nothing but the needs of the audience." But can you really create theater without referring to some other theater?*

SL: That's a beautiful question. I've never thought of that. I've always thought of working in a vacuum. But in that vacuum, of course, I have my training and my training was a very particular special training. I was trained as a director, but also well versed in theater history, Artaud, Brecht... And these would be all in my toolbox if I wanted to use them. I wasn't trained to be a writer—I was actually forced to become a writer. I had no idea I would become a playwright. I had hoped I would be able to direct because I considered myself able to do so. But direct what? There was nothing. There weren't even many translations. Places like Hong Kong and Singapore would develop their theater culture through translations.

SC: I see.

SL: For me, that wasn't the way to go. I said, "We have to do our own. But what is our own?" And the question "What is our own?" ties in deeply with the questions of our epoch, which are "What does it mean to be Taiwanese? What does it mean to be Chinese? and "What is Chinese language theater?" For us, as I said in that interview, there was no continuity, no cord from the past, because we were not able to access

---

19. The journal of the International Association of Theatre Critics.

Stan Lai (April 2022)

China from the 1930s in which there was a burgeoning theater movement. There was some great playwrights, and we weren't part of that. Their plays were banned in Taiwan. There were no local playwrights. It really was a vacuum—but in my mind the possibilities were limitless.

SC: Yes. When I read that statement of yours, it made me think of what Edward Albee told me when I interviewed him [in Theater Voices by Steve Capra]. He said he wanted a theater that the audience could appreciate without pre-conditions and without making comparisons. That must have been the way the audience reacted to your theater. They weren't expecting Beijing Opera.

SL: Exactly! They didn't know. My first professional work, the fourth work I did through improvisation, is called *That Evening*. We performed at Crosstalk. It's two actors for a whole evening. And what we did was very complicated. There's a Chinese performing art called Crosstalk, and it's basically stand-up comedy. It's very much like Abbott and Costello's routine *Who's on First?* The great Crosstalk routines are like that—that sophisticated, that funny. And political. So it was like in the Qing Dynasty. It was one of the very few ways that Chinese people could laugh and also have some political satire. Perhaps the most famous one is called *The Great Switcheroo*. In it, everyone changes jobs. The conceit is that the Emperor died and all the theaters were closed, so the actors are going to starve. It's all about these famous actors who go to the marketplace and sell vegetables. Nobody buys their vegetables, so they have to sing—because they're all Chinese Opera singers. The people say, "Oh, that's so-and-so!" and they create a big crowd of people. It's funny, it's sad. It's all about politics and it's all about art.

We have these beautiful routines from the past and this whole tradition died out in Taiwan. So I worked with two actors. We didn't want to revive it. We just said, "Let's inform our audience that Crosstalk has died." What is our attitude as intellectuals to the death of Crosstalk? Crosstalk's death is only indicative of many things that are dying every day. What we did was to recreate routines from different periods in history that would reflect that period's, political and social and cultural things. And so it was Crosstalk, but it was Crosstalk done within the context and structure of a full-length play.

SC: Yes.

SL: So the audience—getting back to the audience now—they hadn't seen Crosstalk in years. They had never seen a modern play. So what were their expectations? Who knows, right?

Stan Lai (April 2022)

SC: You mentioned politics. Many directors say that all theater is political at some level. Do you agree with that? Your plays such as Secret Love in Peach Blossom Land, *are they political in any sense?*

SL: Well, what's your definition of political? You could say, "Oh, an entertainment for the King Louis XIV at Versailles—that can't be political." Of course it can. A ballet by Lully or Monier—that can be totally political. It depends how you define it. The important thing is whether the *intent* is political or not. Is there any intention for me to politicize an issue? I find in American theater these days, it seems quite necessary to do that.

SC: Absolutely. Everything is politicized in this country now.

SL: *Look Who's Crosstalking Tonight* is political because it's got a guy from China and a guy from Taiwan, and they're crosstalking on stage for a whole evening. That was done in 1989 and over thirty years later we redid it in Taipei. We were so astonished to find that nothing had changed. The politics, everything we were laughing at and satirizing in 1989, was pretty much the same.

Some of my early plays were very political in nature, and all of my early plays dealt with politics in some way. In fact these plays were part of the movement that led to democracy in Taiwan in the later 1980s. From 1995 to 1997 I wrote and directed a daily—Monday-through-Friday—hour-long sitcom based on events of the day, like *Doonesbury* as a sitcom, called *All in This Family Are Humans*. I used theater actors, and this alternative TV show actually had very good ratings and a loyal following. I wrote and directed over 250 episodes. After that, I started to shun politics, turning inward. I no longer believed that a government should or could be in control of an individual's happiness—at least they probably wouldn't do a very good job—and that the individual must first define that happiness or goal in life, and then secure the means to achieve that through individual effort. My focus shifted to the personal, inward, and spiritual. So my thoughts became more like "it's not so much about what is allotted to you, but how you accept it, and life as it unfolds for you." *A Dream Like a Dream* was the play that most describes this inward change.

Of course you can't escape politics in my later plays like *Mumble Jumble* and *The Village*, but you can see how this shift has moved the perspective toward the inside. My most recent play, *River/Cloud* has this line: "Destiny works in objective ways; but one's well-being is subjective."

SC: In light of the fact that there are film and television in the world, can theater ever again have the importance that it had for Shakespeare's audience, for Ibsen's audience, Shaw's audience?

SL: Emphatically, *yes*. I'm a firm believer in theater because I know what it means to be in a room where the performers and the audience are in the same room breathing the same air and living the same experience. There's no way you can beat something like the ancient Greeks at the Dionysus Festival because it's a moment where the whole society is together hashing out issues.

Unfortunately, in America, this whole thing about theater has become sort of—you used the word "fringe" [in a previous conversation]. But it should be *in the middle*. In Chinese, we say, "dazhong and xiaozhong" ["大眾" and "小眾"]—*the big general public* and *the little general public*. Theater is for the little general public.

But that doesn't mean it's any less influential. The Chinese audience is very young. You play *A Dream Like a Dream* or *Peach Blossom Land* and it's something you can talk about with your friends, something that is different and richer than all the other things you can see. That's why it can create a richer experience than the things for the masses in general.

It's a strange thing that theater has moved to the fringe in America. Theater is like the *life pulse* of a society. A Chinese doctor takes your pulse to see your whole makeup and how your health is. Theater is the pulse. If you take Elizabethan's' pulse in England—very strong. If you take the Greeks in Athens—very strong. What about America today? It's a funny pulse giving you different sorts of messages. It's strong in its own way. It's very proud. Is it losing audience or gaining audience? Is there a Broadway and then there's something else?

SC: Well, that's the problem. Broadway and the fringe are split. They seem to be in two different worlds.

SL: So there you have it. There's a schizophrenic sort of character to the American theater today which reflects on American society.

In China it's hard to tell now. The last few years have not been very good because the censorship has been much stricter. We enjoyed quite a few years of very little censorship.

Caitríona McLaughlin (May 2022)

"It's very important for female directors at the moment that we look at how females are represented in traditional text and not just get annoyed by it, but take ownership over how they're played and presented."

Caitríona McLaughlin (May 2022)

Caitríona McLaughlin was appointed artistic director of the Abbey Theatre, Dublin, in 2020, after having served as associate director since 2017. She received a Clore Fellowship in 2007 and she's worked extensively developing and directing plays in New York and London as well as in Dublin. Her work includes directing for the Irish National Opera and the Wexford Opera. She was named Best Director at the Irish Theatre Awards for her work on the Abbey's production of Marina Carr's play On Raftery's Hill. *Her other work for the Abbey includes directing Roddy Doyle's play* Two Pints, *which toured internationally.*

Steve Capra: *Caitríona, on the Abbey Theatre website you say, "My journey as artistic director begins with two questions. Who were we and who are we now?" And The Irish Times quotes you as saying, "It's important that we're tapping into some political moment or societal moment."*

I understand how we can tap into a political moment through our choice of material. But if the play itself doesn't have a direct political message, if we're doing *A Midsummer Night's Dream* or *Playboy of the Western World,* how can we explore politics?

Caitríona McLaughlin: My feeling is that there's always a way to look at the impulse of the play and to respond to a current political question or societal question with casting, with framing, with context in terms of the set design—music in particular. There's always a way to make a comment or to reframe something.

What I'm most interested in is shifting the focus of the play towards a character that's maybe technically less interesting, that's not one of the main characters. So, for example, at the moment I'm working on *Translations* [by Brian Friel], and there's a character in that who doesn't speak. She represents Ireland in many readings of the play and the impact of Britain on Ireland at the time when they were wiping out the language. But in working on *Translations* I felt there was a way to open up that idea of who's voiceless, who's not seen, who doesn't speak, and at the same time keep it true to the impulse that Friel had, which was the impact of a colonizer on a weaker nation.

The way [Friel] presented Sarah in *Translations,* he describes her as timid. He describes her as fearful. His stereotyping of female gender in that context isn't necessarily the most helpful way to explore the theme of who is left voiceless by oppression or by violence or by aggression. So without changing a word of the play, without changing anything—how that character responds, how that character presents herself—we cast an Egyptian actress. There's a lot of scientific research into how

Caitríona McLaughlin (May 2022)

Irish people are not originally Celtic, but they have this genetic root in Egypt. There's been finds and ancient burial sites that connect Ireland with Egypt. I was really interested in what that meant and in the sound of Arabic music and how it leans into the same world of sound as Irish Celtic music. So by having her sing in Arabic in a scene change in a way that expresses an internal life that's not a spoken life, I was able to open the play up to a wider global context, to discuss oppression.

It's very important for female directors at the moment that we look at how females are represented in traditional text and not just get annoyed by it, but take ownership over how they're played and presented.

SC: Yes, that's very helpful. I've talked with several people about this, and one of them was Glenda Jackson when she was an MP. She said something very interesting. She said, "I've never read a good fascist play." I agreed with her then, but now I remember that Shakespeare was a monarchist and Molière was a monarchist. We—or I, for one—identify political theater with progressive theater. Is there good conservative theater? And is there political theater that discusses rather than proselytizes?

CM: That is a really good question. When Dominic Cooke came into the Royal Court he wanted to give opportunities to young writers like Polly Stenham to write about middle-class Britain. But they wrote about money, about financial worries, about family dynamics. I don't suppose they wrote about big, sort of conservative themes.

I think fascists aren't really interested in theater. I suppose fascist theater is, in essence, the Nuremberg rallies, torchlit processions, tank park salutes, that kind of thing. It's theater as spectacle, but it's not drama. It's pageantry. It's architecture. It's bombastic, because it's not about people, about individuals. But it's an interesting question.

I don't know about fascist plays, but maybe that conservatism in theater where a situation is sort of turned upside down—the normal order of things, as it were—and in the course of the play that some kind of status quo is returned to once threatened—is seen as non-progressive. Maybe that's oversimplifying it, I don't know. But, drama, or my understanding of it, interrogates not just form, but the systems that govern us. Whether that's the Catholic Church, the family unit, or whatever. Where does power sit, and how is it being used?

I think drama shows us how people make decisions and what the outcome of those decisions are. Even if they think they're not political decisions, they're informed by the culture that the play operates in,

Caitríona McLaughlin (May 2022)

and all culture *is* political. Drama shows the mechanisms of that, but in a way that an audience can identify with, because plays are about the relationships between things—of people to other people, to society, to work, to their environment, or whatever it is.

SC: How can I present political theater that discusses? I'd like to produce a political theater that discusses but doesn't proselytize. Have you seen it? Have you ever produced it? I don't know of many plays that directly discuss politics instead of proselytizing and propagandizing.

CM: I think the James Graham plays do discuss politics in a really interesting way, because they show the working of Parliament and all the back-stairs machinations that keep the show on the road. They show the whips and the private secretaries as the stage managers of Westminster. If you go to the factory, you're curious about how things are made, and those plays sort of show how the sausages are made. I haven't produced anything myself. There's a writer in Ireland called Jimmy McAleavey, and he is interesting. He writes plays about Northern Ireland. He sets up a question and then leaves it for the audience. He might establish a number of Republican characters and then leave the audience to decide were they right or were they wrong. *Monster, Dinosaurs, Ghosts* is an interesting example of that.

Colin Murphy wrote a play called *The Treaty* that was performed in Ireland this year, and it was about the signing of the Treaty of Ireland. It was a really interesting example of what you're talking about. In truth, it leaned a little bit in favor of the Irish perspective, but not very much. What it did was to present all the players involved in that political moment—both sides—in a balanced way. There's a big political question here. Were they right to sign the treaty and bring about the partition of Ireland or not? And the entire history of Irish politics since then is based on that moment.

We're at a moment now where the Sinn Féin Party's popularity is rising in Ireland, and where we're questioning our political system. It was really interesting to see this play because it offered both perspectives. The audience were left in a space where they were able to think about whether or not they made the right decision in terms of signing the treaty, whether or not they were in a fair negotiation with the British at the time. It put a question to an audience and left you in a space where you came home thinking about it. That to me, was a very successful piece of work.

We have just recently produced *Three Monologues* by Jennifer

Caitríona McLaughlin (May 2022)

Johnston, and these three monologues offer both perspectives of the 1980s, at the height of the Northern Irish conflict. There are three characters that are not directly involved in the conflict. One is a wife of a Republican prisoner. One is a wife of a man who was shot—he was part of the paramilitaries. He was shot by Republicans. And then the third is a Unionist man living his whole life on his family farm, and he actually himself gets shot. There are three different perspectives on the conflict and three characters, all with a different background. When the three are presented together like that, it leaves the audience in a challenging space where everybody's right and nobody's wrong.

These political pieces are the closest that come to mind in terms of what you're talking about. It's been grist to the mill for Irish writers, the conflict and the aftermath of the conflict. And the Civil War anniversary is next year—100 years since the Civil War here. So there is quite a bit of that.

There's a couple of plays of the kind of [Peter Morgan's] *Frost/Nixon* model that are more political and were written in the UK, where it's like a conversation, where it goes to and fro.

Stewart Parker, the Northern Irish playwright, is another one who wrote plays that left you in a space where you as an audience decided whose side or what perspective to take.

SC: That's very helpful.

Four years ago in your keynote speech at the Theater Forum Conference, you talked about the inequality in the way theater treats the regions. I was happy to hear you say that, because in America, where theater is very centralized, that's also a problem. Could you say more about that? You said you're not sure how we could change it—can you give me some ideas about that?

CM: Yeah. There's a snobbery around the kind of work that gets made in the regions. It's partly because of how funding is dispersed, particularly in Ireland. One of the problems is that in Ireland there's a couple of major cities, but the rest of Ireland is very rural and it has very poor public transport. So it's not viable for artists to make their lives in much of rural Ireland and have enough work to sustain themselves.

There's a whole combination of social reasons why people haven't been encouraged to stay in those places and work. It tends to be amateurs, people who do it alongside other day jobs. It's really frustrating because in Ireland there is a massive, thriving amateur drama world. There's competitions all the time. At the Abbey we host the winner of one of them, but they're all over the country. The talent is there, the interest is there, but there's not enough money for people to actually develop careers there.

The other thing that happens here is that we have a tendency to put money into buildings and not people. A lot of buildings were put into places around the country twenty-odd years ago to celebrate the new millennium and nobody thought about how to keep artists in those buildings or how to develop sustainable opportunities for young artists coming up. There'd be youth theater, there'd be amateur drama, there'd be visiting companies—but there's nothing that actually grows at the grassroots level.

And I do think there's a little bit of snobbery about rural Ireland—misguided, I will say, being a countrywoman myself.

SC: *That's true in the States as well. But I think that the Irish are probably more educated to theater than Americans.*

CM: Well, it's a fundamental part of our schooling, drama, the writers and literary history of the country. Education was always a big part of Irish identity and Irish culture. People quote Shakespeare here. You can hear people quoting Sean O'Casey on public transport, or Yeats. It's part of everyday speech here. So I suppose you are right in that way.

SC: *In that case I'll get there as soon as I can!*

SC: *Caitríona, I just have one more question. In light of the fact that there are film and television in the world, can theater ever again have the importance of Shakespeare's audience, or for Ibsen's audience.*

CM: You know what? I think it's *more* important because of that. I don't think we realize how valuable the shared experience of sitting in an audience together—having our hearts beat at the same time, breathing the same air, and deciding on what we think about what's in front of us in a shared, dark space—is for how we engage with the world, for our own humanity, for our understanding of ourselves.

Covid has really heightened the importance of live, shared spaces and live, shared art forms. Theater is definitely going through a change. The ideas inside the text are not going to have the same discussion points that they did or cause controversial conversations around the country—or not for a couple of years anyway. But coming into a space where we're all thinking about what's in front of us and trying to understand ourselves and how we feel about ourselves and about each other in the context of what's going on is more important than ever.

Caitríona McLaughlin (May 2022)

Do you know *An Octoroon*, an American play by Branden Jacobs-Jenkins? It's a fascinating play. We have put it on.

SC: I think it's based on [Dion] Boucicault [1820–1890].

CM: It *is* based on Boucicault. Boucicault was born around the corner from the Abbey and was obsessed with how the Irish stereotype was presented in British theater. When he wrote *The Octoroon*, he was trying to explore the question of slavery in America, and he did it in a typically ham-fisted, clumsy way, in Victorian words. Branden Jacobs-Jenkins has responded to this play with an extraordinary framing device that uses the play to look at how we stereotype black culture, how we create characters in popular culture drawn on images, thoughts, ideas, language, rhythms that have no basis in reality.

We put this play on with a majority of black actors, a majority of whom are from Ireland. Not everyone is—the director came from the UK and two of the actors came from the UK. But it's a watershed moment for us in terms of the kind of theater that is relevant and the characters that are relevant. To be able to have a conversation with an Irish audience about racism at the moment, in such a public way, is very, very new. I know we're way behind America and the UK, but we have such a different relationship to race because of our own history and our own colonized position. It's got five-star reviews almost across the board. People have responded with enormous positivity. Putting it on today has started a conversation in Dublin that I didn't think I would hear for a very long time.

Theater still has a really vital role to play in helping us understand who our society is. It went through a kind of existential crisis during covid, and we all were afraid we were going to have to live in the digital world from here on. But now we're having to reset who we were and who we are now. We're having to re-question, re-examine, re-think those things.

Theater like this—theater that has new voices and new perspectives in it, that has new energy, new music, new dance in it—is incredibly exciting and reinvigorating and how it is the starting place for a whole new wave of theater.

SC: That's very encouraging. I'm happy to hear you say that.

CM: Well, I'm a passionate believer in the importance of theater. The importance of theater is to help us understand what we think when we're sitting there listening to people laugh at something we find offensive, or laughing ourselves at something that turns into something dark and challenging. It's really, really interesting, valuable and essential for our well-being.

Robert Icke (August 2022)

"Theater is not an art form in the same health that it was in 1599. It's not essential to the culture. We've been bad guardians of it."

Robert Icke was appointed Ibsen Artist in Residence at International Theater Amsterdam in 2019. He had previously been associate director of the Almeida Theatre and artistic director of both the Arden Theatre Company and the Swan Theatre Company (all UK). Noted internationally for his bold adaptations of classics, he's received many honors, including two Evening Standard *Best Director Awards, the Critics Circle Award, the Kurt Hübner Award and the Olivier Award. He is a Fellow of the Royal Society of Literature. This interview took place while Icke's productions of* Hamlet *and* Oresteia *were running in New York.*

Steve Capra: *In adapting* Hamlet, *you used text from the first folio and the first and second quartos. What principle did you use when you selected material from each?*

Robert Icke: With *Hamlet*, there is no authorized version. There are three versions. And the principle, for me, is one of going, "How can I deliver the play in its ultimate, in its most essential form, to an audience now?" And the word *now* is the most important. Even if I could recreate for us exactly, to the letter, the *Hamlet* that was performed in 1599, I can't create for you what it would feel like to be in London in 1599. I can't make you feel whatever it must have felt like to be in a country that had been Catholic for many years, then Protestant under Henry VIII, then *really* Protestant under his son, then Catholic again under his daughter, and then sort of Protestant again. But I do know that when Dad Hamlet's ghost turns up and says he's in Purgatory, that must have spiked something in the contemporary audience, the 1599 audience, that now it doesn't.

And so it's the double question of going "What is this thing trying to do?" and also "What is this play now? When released into the wilds of *now*, how does it live?"

Robert Icke (August 2022)

Some of that is just a taste question of going, "Okay, what do we prefer of *sullied* and *solid?*" Sometimes it's balance. Cutting is often an intuitive thing where one thinks "Okay, rhythmically, it feels like we could do with a little bit less, or maybe we could do a bit more." One is loath to cut much from a character like Ophelia who you're desperate to have more of. It all stays with Gertrude because you're not going to throw away any of the breadcrumbs that you have.

Sometimes it's dramaturgical—I'm thinking there of the scene that I include, the Gertrude–Horatio scene, which for me solves a huge problem I've had every time I've seen that play, which is the *pirate* bit. You just think, "I'm not sure if I've ever followed that." If it's not *gettable* by a contemporary audience on a first hearing, then I try to find a way that clarifies it. I don't mean everything; I just mean narrative clarity. What is happening in the play? What is the tension of the story at this point? That's the cluster of things in my mind as I read and prepare and open as many questions as I can.

SC: *I was happy to read that you've been critical of the theater, calling it boring—and also of critics, calling them shallow. In this country at least, everyone's very hesitant to be critical, even critics. Does this explain why you do so many adaptations?*

RI: The history of classical theater is really a history of adaptation. What the Greeks are doing is taking stories that are present in myth and in Homer—and changing them. If you were a classical Athenian going to see *Oedipus*, you would know that Oedipus has a mother called *Jocasta*, who he also sleeps with, and you would expect that the death of his father and the sex with his mother would happen as part of the play's dramatic action—in the same way that when you go to *Medea*, the killing of the kids happens as part of the dramatic action. The joyous shock of it is that Sophocles has had it all happen before the play began and all you're going to watch is them *finding out* that that this is what's happened. That would have been, to an Athenian audience, surprising. "What? This is not what we thought we were coming for."

Shakespeare's doing the same thing. All his plays have sources and some of them have plays. *King Leir* is a play owned by that company with a happy ending that he takes and he rewrites, extensively changes. The effect of that must have been that people in the audience who knew the old play had that feeling of going "Wait, what? Like, this is not what happens in this play. This is not King Leir." The modern idea that there

Robert Icke (August 2022)

are new plays and then there are adaptations and that those two things are distinct from each other is a modern idea.

SC: Yes.

RI: For me, one of the great things about theater is that it allows one to hold together the very, very old and the very, very new. The actors are speaking *live* in front of you tonight. But in another sense, when at the beginning of *Oresteia*, Michael [Abubakar, playing Calchas] speaks the word "Θεοὺς" [Theoús], which is the first word of the *Oresteia* in Greek, he's beginning a ritual with the same word that would have been used to begin that same ritual 2,500 years ago. And so we're doing something very, very old but also very, very new.

I've never really bought into the idea that there are right ways to do these plays. I think the right way changes with time. I've had the experience with a production I made, *The Doctor*. It's an adaptation of an Arthur Schnitzler play called *Professor Bernhardi*, which thinks about medical ethics, identity politics, racial justice and abortion. Abortion didn't feel like a particularly hot topic in society in 2019. The role in society of a doctor didn't feel like a hot topic in society in 2019. Post-pandemic, now it does. Post–Black Lives Matter, the question of racial identity and racial justice feels much more present. I've watched a thing that I made change its meaning because time has passed.

So the idea that there is a kind of a *way* to do *Hamlet* I find false. I think there is only a way to do *Hamlet now*. In another few months It'll be somebody else's turn and the right way will be a different way—and depending on where you are. If you're performing in Belarus, that's going to be different. If you're performing in London it's going to be different.

I don't have a general disrespect for critics. I think critics can be incredibly useful. I think they should be a huge part of the ecosystem of how a healthy theater culture works.

SC: Thank you.

RI: But they can also be very damaging because they can be the guardians of—well, we call it a *revival* when we do an old play, which means to take something dead and bring it back to life. And so often the *revival* is not a revival. We sort of sit the corpse up and we put face paint on it. Very often critics are the guardians of the deadly. And they say, "You can't do that. That's not allowed."

The true critic, the critic who is really in dialogue with the work, when you offer them that, through the production, says, "Interesting. I'm not sure I agree with you, but I'm interested." Whereas the deadly critic will say, "No, no, no, you're wrong. There is a right way to do this play. And this is not that." Often what they're saying is, "This is not the version I saw when I was 15 and fell in love with." That's understandable—but they're not present in the room.

When people give you notes, they're often presenting you with a *solution*. What you want to be presented with is a *problem*. Somebody will say, "I think Steve should wear a pink hat." And I'll say, "Okay, so you've offered me a solution, but what is the problem you're articulating? You're saying that you think his costume is not vivid enough and that his costume should be more *out there*." The solution is boring and easy to reject—because I go "Well, I don't want a pink hat," and I dismiss it. But within the offer of a solution is the diagnosis of a problem.

Gertrude can't see the ghost of old King Hamlet. Does this mean the ghost isn't there? Perhaps. And so solution offers us the way back to a problem, which is "What if that ghost only exists in Hamlet's mind? What does that mean for our reading of everything else that happens in the play?" Shakespeare offers you contradictory evidence.

One of the things I like best about *Othello* is at the end when Iago says, "What you know, you know," and one thinks "What's that, though? What do I know about what I've been watching?" This collapsing of ambiguity and ambivalence into certainty is part of the reason why the production history of that play has largely been a racist one—because in a production where Desdemona is *definitely* innocent, Othello becomes a bit foolish. Whereas if Iago spots something that he thinks might really be there, the whole thing gets more complicated.

SC: There's always that ambiguity, yes.

RI: Which Shakespeare is full of. I find it very inspiring, that bit in *Hamlet* about the mirror being held up to nature. He's riffing on what is the purpose of playing, and he says "to hold ... the mirror up to nature ... to show ... the very age and body of the time his form and pressure." I'm interested in that *age and body*. What does he want to show, "the age and body of the time"? He wants to show its form and pressure. You think, "Okay, what is the form of the time we live in? If one had to make a shape out of it, what would be its shape? And then if you had to fill up that shape with pressure, what would be its pressure?" I don't really understand that line, but it's lovely, isn't it? It offers you a lovely thing about going "What is the pressure of 2022? What is the form? How can we show you those things?"

Robert Icke (August 2022)

Everything contradicts itself. Shakespeare goes so far in one direction that the opposite then becomes implied. And often the opposite is stated in the play. You watch Hamlet see a ghost and then a bit later in "To be or not to be," he's talking about "The undiscover'd country, from whose bourn / No traveller returns—." And one thinks "Well, you've just seen a traveler return." One of the reasons I find the play so moving is that it doesn't solve any of those things.

One of the discoveries for me was that Hamlet tries to make one more soliloquy at the end when he says: "You that look pale and tremble at this chance,/That are but mutes or audience to this act,/Had I but time,—O I could tell you."

What could you tell us now you know you're dying? You began the play by saying you wished your flesh would melt. Now your flesh is melting. What could you tell us now that you couldn't tell us before? But he doesn't tell us—he simply says, "But let it be." And you think, "Oh, wow, it's so beautiful!"—and yet you never *get* it. Or at least I never got it because I'm always watching someone do some realist version of what it means to die. I'd never heard what the writing *is*.

The first step to solving any problem is to admit that there is one. Theater is not an art form in the same health that it was in 1599. It's not essential to the culture. We've been bad guardians of it.

SC: Which brings me to my next question. In light of the fact that there are television and film in the world, can theater ever have that importance again that it had for Shakespeare's audience?

RI: Yeah. It could. The challenges are profound—the first one being the price of the ticket. If I could change one thing, that's what I would change. If you were paying the same as you pay to go to the cinema, it wouldn't matter. But when you're having to invest the price of a new jacket in one ticket, well, then no wonder you want to go and see *Hamilton*, which definitely works, rather than take a risk on something that might not work. As anybody knows who's been around the process of making a play, it's really *hard*. And a lot of the time it doesn't work. You can't get it to do what you want it to do, and it doesn't quite happen and circumstances happen, as we've had on this production, that make it really *tough* to get up the mountain.

If I ever had to run a theater, which I hope I never have to do, the thing would be to divorce entirely box office income from the producing model. So you'd say, "We will budget for selling zero tickets. We'll seek funding, but we're not going to need money from the box office."

Robert Icke (August 2022)

Which will mean that we can go "Okay, who would we like to invite? Is it schoolchildren?"

A lot of my work is made often imagining two people—a 13- or 14-year-old who knows nothing about *Hamlet*, who doesn't know what happens in *Hamlet*; and, at the same time, a world expert.

Often the critic is in an incredibly difficult position. They're invited to *Two Noble Kinsmen*. They may have never read that play, but they're in a position where they feel like they must be expert. To become expert on a Shakespeare play is a lifetime's work, and yet they have to sit in judgment, tonight, at this and assess it. Unless you have seen *Noble Kinsmen* and you've spent time with that play, it's really tough to come in and assess what's happening with this text and this group of people.

And the critic in the middle of that Venn diagram is very difficult to please because they know a little—and a little knowledge is a dangerous thing. An audience member who is completely virginal—I should be able to captivate them. And someone who knows *everything* about the play, well they will see what we're up to, even if they hate it, because they know the territory. It's the middle of that that can be very tricky.

SC: *Yes, my knowledge of* The Oresteia *got in the way when I saw that your* Oresteia *was not* The Oresteia *that I've read. Once I got over that, I was much more at ease.*

RI: And that's an interesting thing, isn't it? How can I disarm you of the baggage you bring? It's much easier for me to hit my 14-year-old audience member who knows nothing because I can curate their first journey through the material.

And then there's the ambiguity. Shakespeare is really alive to the sort of *is/isn't* quality of theater all the time. You know it's not real. You know Polonius doesn't really die, but also you're in a suspended state where he is real and he does die. And maybe you'll cry real tears, even though you know it's not real.

To answer your question "Can theatre still be alive? Can it still survive?": nothing else can quite do that doubleness. Nothing else is live in front of you in that way.

SC: *The New Statesman, of all magazines, quoted David Benedict as saying that you appear to be on a mission but he doesn't know what that mission is. Do you want to respond to that?*

RI: I've never met David Benedict, so I don't know where he got that from. I'd be interested to know what his evidence is for that, what the thought is. The work anybody makes is at the mercy of lots of things.

Robert Icke (August 2022)

You can only make the choices of the things you're asked to do. Sometimes people react to the decisions artists make and say, "But why would they do that?" As if we can knock on the door of the National Theatre and say, "Hello, I would like to now do this. Roll out the carpet, please."

But the choices I make as an artist are the invitations I have. Ivo van Hove said to me, "Come and make work in Dutch, [at International Theater] Amsterdam." I wasn't on a mission to make work in Dutch, but he offered me an amazing ensemble of actors and the keys to the car and said, "I want you to come and make what you want to make. The condition is it has to be made with these people and these people act in Dutch." And I wouldn't have missed that for the world.

Afterword

What are we to make of all this? Certainly, the height and depth and breadth of our theater is apparent—and we're infinitely grateful for that range. But Robert Icke tells us that we've been "bad guardians" of the theater, while Andre Bishop tells us "we're living in a golden age of American theater."

Can theater ever again be as important as it was for Ibsen's audience? Kip Williams' and Stan Lai's answers are emphatically positive, but Richard Eyre and Michael Blakemore are, equally emphatically, pessimistic.

We certainly don't have a snapshot of a generation here. When I interviewed Judith Malina, she was old enough to be the grandmother of many of other directors—and her work was still radical.

Malina tells us that only political theater can be elevating, but Oskaras Koršunovas calls political theater "boring." Jorge Vargas isn't sure that theater has a social effect at all and Stan Lai tells us that the important thing is whether the *intent* of the work is political.

What of the complexity of the dramaturgy—its use, for example, of electronic media? Kip Williams is much celebrated for his use of video; John Doyle's minimalist production of *Peer Gynt* was pared down to actors alone. Ivo van Hove, for that matter, has been called a "maximalist minimalist."

What of theater's relationship to its audience? Richard Eyre's production of *The Marriage of Figaro* stayed formally behind the proscenium. Marc Caellas—in a breathtaking gesture of intimacy—has offered his audience cocaine.

And what of verisimilitude? Much of Ping Chong's theater is *actualism;* Robert Wilson's hallucinatory expressionism scarcely looks at all like life at all.

Whatever questions we approach this book with, we do not find herein "an answer." We find several answers. We are, after all, talking about the inexpressible. Each director holds the mirror up to nature in

Afterword

their own way. Without attempting to lead the reader, I'd like to point out André Bishop's statement that the role of the artistic director is to exercise his own taste.

As articulate as these artists are, I'm sure they'd all agree that it's the *event* of theater that's important, not its *discussion*. I hope that, at the very least, this Afterword encourages the reader to drop this book and go to the theater.

—Steve Capra

Index

Abbey Theatre 136ff
Abbot and Costello 133
Albee, Edward 133
All in This Family Are Humans 134
Almodovar, Pedro 67
Alys, Francis 90
Amarillo 81ff
American Place Theater 64, 65
Angels in America 35
Animations 26
Antic Theatre 86
Archer, William 5
Arena Theater 31
Arguments with England 102
Aristotle 116
Ars Nova 65
The Art of the Theater: Then and Now 59
Artaud, Antoine 22, 56, 121
August: Osage County 9

Balanchine, George 25
Banos Roma 82
The Barber of Seville 70
Barker, Harley Granville 5
Beck, Julian 98
Beckett, Samuel 111
Beijing Opera 133
Benedict, David 147
Bentley, Eric 35
Berliner Ensemble 28
Billington, Michael 104
Blind Boys of Alabama 31
Blithe Spirit 101
Blowjob 97
Boal, August 122
bobrauschenbergamerica 42
Book of Mormon 34
Boucicault, Dion 141
Brant, George 44
Brantley, Ben 92
Bread and Puppet Theater 12ff
Brecht, Bertolt 18, 28, 35ff, 37, 114, 123
Brief Interviews with Repulsive Men 89
Britten, Benjamin 55

Brook, Peter 19, 56, 109, 111, 113
Brustein, Robert 103
Bunraku 46
Burstein, Danny 71
Bye, Mister 122

Cariolan 28
Cats 43
Chau Misterix 122
Chekhov, Anton 38ff
Chewing Gum Dreams 117
Chinese Opera 55, 133
Churchill, Caryl 115
Circle Repertory Theater 65
Cirque du Soleil 109, 111
Ciudad Juarez 82
Clair Tow Theater 61
Classic Stage 50, 53
La Clemenza di Tito 55
Club Thumb 65
Cocteau, Jean 107
Coel, Michaela 117
The Color Purple 48ff, 51, 53ff
Comédie-Française 93
Cooke, Dominic 137
Coward, Noel 101
Crosstalk 133
Curlew River 55

The Damned 92ff, 112
Davis, Miles 107
A Day in the Life of Joe Egg 100
Democracy in Mexico 76ff
The Dictionary of Soul 73, 75ff
Dirty Dancing 12
Disney Studios 29, 46
Disneyworld 29
La Divina 29ff
The Divine Reality Circus Comedy 15
The Doctor 144
Doll House 28
A Doll's House 28
Doonesbury. 134
A Dream Like a Dream 134, 135

151

Index

Einstein one the Beach 25
Entrevistas breves con escritores repulsivos 89
Etherege, George 10
Eustis, Oskar 37, 45

Factory 2 96
Fiddler on the Roof 67
Foreman, Richard 27
Freeman, Morgan 31
Friedman, Thomas 41
Friel, Brian 136
Frost/Nixon 139
Fugard, Athol 18

Garneau, Michel 108
Generation NYZ 57
Gilbert, Morris 79
The Girl in the Yellow Dress 17, 20
Glass, Philip 25
Goldenthal, Elliot 45
Gospel at Colonus 30
Graham, James 138
Green Bird 45
Grounded 44ff
Group Theater 37, 103
Guetell, Adam 69
Guys and Dolls 34

Hall, Peter 35, 103, 120
Hamilton 117
Hamlet 36, 142ff
Hare, David 7, 35
Harris, Jeremy O. 117
Hathaway, Anne 45
Henry V 9
H.G. 24
History Boys 8, 10, 12

I May Destroy You 117
Ibsen, Henrik 35, 118
Icke, Robert 113
The Importance of Being Ernest 10
Intiman Theatre 71
Ivo van Hove: From Shakespeare to David Bowie 90

Jackson, Glenda 137
Jacobs-Henkins, Branden 117, 141
Johnston, Jennifer 138
Juan Darien 45
Judd, Donald 25
Julia 127
Julius Caesar 115

Kafka, Franz 97
Kaputt 98
The King and I 71

King Leir 143
Korach 22
Kosky, Barrie 113
Krannert Center 42
Kushner, Tony 36, 37

La MaMa ETC 29, 60, 64, 68, 73, 74
Lahr, John 105
Lansbury, Angela 101
Lecoq, Jacques 106
Levine, James 33
The Lexus and the Olive Tree 41
The Life 105
Lincoln Center Theater 60ff, 66ff
The Lingering Now 127
Lion King 43ff
Living Newspaper 37
Living Theater 21ff, 27, 68, 96, 103
London Road 34
London Theatre (magazine) 105
Long Day's Journey into Night 101
Look Who's Crosstalking Tonight 134
Lord of the Flies 115
Lori-Parks, Suzi 37
Love and Information 115
Lully, Jean-Baptiste 134

M, Lego 47
Mabou Mines 27
Macbeth 108
The Magic Flute 45
Mahabharata 47
Malaparte, Curzi 98
Malina, Judith 27, 98, 103, 106
The Man of Mode 10
Manhattan Theater Club 65
Mann, Emily 37
Market Theatre 17ff
The Marriage of Figaro 31, 33
McAleavey, Jimmy 138
McLuhan, Marshall 39, 83
The Medium 38
Metropolitan Opera 31, 45, 71
Michelangelo 98
Midsummer Night's Dream 46, 136
Miller, Arthur 36
Ministry Department of Arts and Culture, S. Africa 21
Miranda, Lin-Manuel 117
Miss Julie 113, 127
Miss Saigon 8, 10
Mitchell, Katie 12
Molière 137
Monier, Georges 134
Monk, Meredith 56
Monsters, Dinosaurs, Ghosts 138
More Stately Mansions 39
Morgan, Peter 139

Index

Mumble Jumble 134
Murphy, Colin 138
My Fair Lady 60, 61, 67ff

National Arts Council, S. Africa 21
National Endowment for the Arts 15, 30
National Festival of the Arts, S. Africa
National Theatre, London 5ff
Needles and Opium 107
Network 92
New York Theater Workshop 39
Nichols, Peter 100, 101
Nietzsche, Friedrich 29
Noises Off 101

O'Casey, Sean 140
An Octoroon 141
The Odyssey 127
Oedipus Rex 143
O'Hara, Kelly 71
Old Vic 103
Olivier, Laurence 9, 103
O'Neill, Eugene 39
Oresteia 144, 147
Osborne, John 101
Oslo 67
Othello 145

Paradise Now 22
Parker, Stewart 139
The Parties 25
El paseo de Robert Walser 86ff
Passion 50
Peer Gynt 25, 48ff
Pequeños Territorios en Reconstrucción 83
El perico tumba la paloma 88
The Picture of Dorian Gray 113, 115, 118
Piscator, Edward 22
The Playboy of the Western World 136
Playwrights Horizons 64
The Pragmatists 99
Prince, Harold 120
Professor Bernhardi 144
Public Theater 64

Quinones, Edison 88, 89

Radio Macbeth 42
Ramayana 47
Ratatouille 10
Reich, Steve 93
Richardson, Ralph 103
Rigoletto 66, 69
River/Cloud 134
Royal National Theatre 5ff, 11, 12, 53, 103
Royal Shakespeare Company 53, 103
Rude Mechanicals 30

Sacco and Vanzetti 122, 123
Schall, Ekkehard 28
Schnitzler, Arthur 144
Scottish National Theatre 6
Secret Love in Peach Blossom Land 131ff
Shaggy Dog Animation 30
Shakespeare, William 33ff, 45, 66, 70, 101, 107ff, 143, 145ff
Shaw, George Bernard 67, 68, 118
Simon, Neil 66
SITI Company 36ff
Slaves 98
Small Territories under Consruction 83
Smith, Maggie 105
So What's New 20
Solanas, Pino 122
some trace of her 12
Sophocles 143
The Sorcerer's Apprentice 28
Sorkin, Aaron 69
Southwark Playhouse 105
Spider-Man 44
Spoleto Festival 55
Stage Blood 102, 103
Stein, Gertrude 37
Stenham, Polly 137
Stephens, Simon 94
Steppenwolf Theater 9
Stoppard, Tom 101
Strindberg, August 127
Stuff Happens 7
Suddenly Last Summer 114
Suzuki 40, 41
Sydney Theatre Company 116, 117

Talking Theater 35, 36
Teartr Stary 96
Teatro Línea de Sombra 81ff
Terrassa Noves Tendències 86
Terrenal. Pequeño misterio ácrata 119
Terrestrial. A Small Anarchist Mystery 119
That Evening 133
Thate, Hilmar 28
Theatre of Cruelty 121
Theater Voices 133
Three Monologues 138
Three Sisters 126ff
Tijuana 76ff
The Time Machine 24
Time Rocker 24
To Kill a Mockingbird 67ff
Toyi-Toyi 19
Translations 136
The Treaty 138
The Trial 97
Twelfth Night 10
Two Noble Kinsmen 147
Tynan, Kenneth 103, 104

Index

Under Milkwood 117
Undesirable Elements 57ff
Utopia 128

van Hove, Ivo 39, 102, 112, 113, 148
Verdi, Giuseppe 66
A View from the Bridge 93, 113
Viewpoints 40, 41
The Village 130, 134
Wagner, Gustav 93

Waiting for Godot 35
The Walk 87
The Walk of Robert Walker 86ff
Wallace, David Foster 89
Warhol, Andy 96
Warrior Ant 30

Watanabe, Ken 71
Wayang Kulit 46ff
Wells, H.G. 24
West Side Story 91ff, 95
What If They Went to Moscow? 126ff
What's the Story: Essays About Art, Theater and Storytelling 37
White, Christian Dante 71
Who's on First 133
William, David 100
Williams, Tennessee 36, 114
Witkiewicz, Stanislaw Ignacy 99
A Woman on the Verge 67
Woza Albert 19

Yasbeck, David 69
Yeats, William Butler 140